MICROWAVE
C O O K I N G
MAIN MEALS

DI BUSSCHAU

PHOTOGRAPHY BY MIKE ROBINSON

NEW
HOLLAND

First published in the UK in 1994 by
New Holland (Publishers) Ltd
37 Connaught Street, London W2 2AZ

ISBN 1 85368 317 5

Editors: Alison Leach and Sandie Vahl
Designer: Petal Palmer
Hand lettering: Andrew van der Merwe
Photographer: Mike Robinson
Stylists: Di Busschau and Helen Lindsey-Clark

Typesetting by Ace Filmsetting Ltd, Frome, Somerset
Reproduction by Unifoto (Pty) Ltd
Printed and bound in Singapore by Tien Wah Press (Pte) Ltd

CONTENTS

·····················

People seldom read the instructions at the beginning of the book, so if you are here with me now, you will have the benefit of using these recipes as successfully as I have.

Over the past fifteen years or so, I have seen how microwaves have revolutionized the kitchens of families, single people, chefs and caterers. They are quick, economical to use, compact, easy to keep clean, and ensure a cool and comfortable cooking environment in hot weather. Above all, food cooked in a microwave is healthy food using less fat and providing us with the nutrients and energy we need to cope with the stresses of modern life.

wave energy, making the base very hot, which then sears and browns the food when it comes into contact with it. Preheat the browning dish according to the manufacturer's instructions. Depending on its size, this will take a maximum of about 8 minutes. Meat should be patted dry with a paper towel, flavoured with herbs or spices and placed immediately in the dish. The dish should not be removed from the microwave until cooking is complete as its base must remain very hot to brown the food and so it must not make contact with any cool surface. The use of butter, oil or margarine in the browning dish depends on personal preference, but may be omitted.

SERVINGS

All recipes in this book serve four, unless specified otherwise. If you *increase* quantities, increase the cooking time proportionally, then *subtract* ⅓ of the total cooking time (for example, 1 baked potato = 4 minutes; 3 baked potatoes = [4 × 3] − 4 = 8 minutes). If you *decrease* quantities, decrease the cooking time proportionally, then *add* ⅓ of the total cooking time (for example, 3 baked potatoes = 8 minutes; 1 baked potato = [8 ÷ 3] + 1⅔ = about 4 minutes).

CONTAINERS

Most types of dishes can be used in the oven, except:
◆ crockery with silver rims;
◆ ordinary Tupperware;
◆ plastic that is not pliable (as with certain plastic jugs);
◆ metal containers.
For combination ovens, use ovenproof cookware and certain types of plastic-ware that is specially manufactured for use in ovens up to 210°C.

BROWNING DISH

The browning dish, manufactured in various forms, is to the microwave what the frying pan is to the hob. The substance in the base of the dish (mica) absorbs micro-

COOKING ON A RACK

When cooking a dish such as a quiche, where you don't want to end up with a soft, undercooked centre, place the dish on a slightly raised rack. This enables the microwaves to cook from underneath the dish.

COVERING FOOD

Generally, for moist cooking (as with vegetables), the container should be covered securely with a lid or cling film. For dry cooking (as with pies), the food should not be covered.

ORDER OF COOKING

When you are preparing a meal, first cook the food that takes the longest to cook (such as rice and meat) as it will have a longer standing time. Vegetables then can be cooked while the meat is standing.

DEFROSTING

All food should be completely defrosted before cooking in a microwave. It is safer to defrost food quickly in a microwave than to leave it over a long period at room temperature as there is considerably less chance of harmful bacteria building up. Also, important nutrients, flavour and moisture are not lost when food is defrosted quickly. Remember that food should be turned or shielded with small pieces of foil to ensure that it defrosts evenly, and it will continue defrosting while standing.

INGREDIENTS

◆ As the metric and imperial quantities given in every recipe are not interchangeable, follow whichever system of measurement you prefer but do not combine them.

◆ The ingredients are listed in the order in which they are used.

◆ Depending on your personal preference or cholesterol count, butter may be replaced by margarine in all the recipes in this book.

◆ Where cream is used, yoghurt may be substituted — it does not curdle in a microwave.

◆ Fresh herbs and freshly ground spices are best for flavour, but dried herbs and pre-packed spices are more convenient to use. Substitute 5 ml/1 teaspoon dried herbs for 15 ml/1 tablespoon fresh.

COMBINATION OVENS

These ovens use a combination of convection and microwave cooking and have become very popular because the results are impressive. Some combination ovens use convection and microwave energy simultaneously, and other types alternate convection and microwave energy. Much shorter cooking times are required with the former.

A quartz grill is now a feature of most combination ovens and even of some compact microwaves, adding a new dimension to microwave cooking. It can be used independently as well as with either microwave power or convection.

COOKING AND STANDING TIMES

Cooking times vary according to the wattage and make of the microwave. All the cooking times given in the recipes are therefore approximate. These recipes were tested in a 650-watt microwave, so if yours has a higher wattage, it is best to use a shorter cooking time initially and then cook for a little longer if necessary.

Food continues to cook for a short time after being removed from a microwave. This is known as standing time. In those recipes where this is an essential part of the cooking process, it is specified.

RADIATION FACTOR

The risk of exposure to radiation through using a microwave is minimal. Microwaves are electromagnetic waves, similar to those that enable us to watch television. The many safety features include a series of locks and seals which make it impossible to operate the microwave without the door being tightly shut. So just relax and enjoy cooking with your microwave!

MICROWAVE POWER LEVELS

A fundamental difference between microwave and conventional cooking is that control is by time rather than by temperature. Instead of temperature settings as in a conventional oven or adjustable controls on the hob, microwaves have variable power levels that control the speed at which food is cooked.

The terms used to describe the degrees of energy are unfortunately not standardized and can be expressed in words, numerals or, occasionally, as a percentage of the total wattage, by different manufacturers. The following list is merely a guideline:

POWER LEVEL	% POWER
Low	25
Defrost	30
Medium-Low	40
Medium	50
Medium-High	60–70
High	100

There is no exact formula for adjusting cooking times when using microwaves of a different power level to the one specified in a particular cookbook. If the recipes have been tested in a 650-watt microwave, as in this book, and your microwave is, for example, 700 watts, it is suggested you take off 10 seconds for every minute and then check.

Most microwave manufacturers supply detailed instructions for using specific models; they usually also have a cookery advice service staffed by experienced home economists who will be able to tell you what adjustments are needed.

Microwaves are frequently used to heat the ready-prepared recipe dishes that are widely available in supermarkets. Some of these in the UK are now labelled Heating Category A, B and so on to denote the microwave power level, in an attempt to introduce standardized descriptions in the EC.

CHAPTER ONE

Seafood

SEAFOOD is a rich source of high-grade protein, with very little fat. Fish and shellfish contain plenty of vitamins and minerals and are succulent and tasty when cooked in the microwave. Try a variety of sauces to jazz seafood up and make the taste buds tingle!

NOTES

◆ Fresh seafood is best for flavour. If you must replace it with frozen, defrost completely before cooking.

◆ Seafood should be cooked for 1 minute per 100 g/ 3½ oz, plus another 3–4 for the sauce. When fish is just cooked, it will be opaque (losing that pinkish-blue colour) and it will flake easily at the thickest end. Shellfish is cooked when the flesh is opaque and just firm, and when the shell turns pink.

◆ Never prepare seafood in advance and then reheat it, as the result will be an overcooked, dried out and tasteless meal. Besides, seafood cooks so quickly in the micro-wave, it isn't necessary to cook in advance.

◆ When preparing a meal, cook the rice and vegetables first, then keep them warm while you prepare the seafood.

SALMON BISQUE

This is a rich and creamy soup that makes use of the convenience of canned seafood and which makes a filling dish for a main meal. A loaf of crusty French bread is the perfect accompaniment.

>   440 g/14 oz canned salmon, drained
>   and flaked
>   2 tomatoes, peeled and chopped
>   1 onion, chopped
>   250 ml/8 fl oz water
>   freshly ground black pepper to taste
>   2.5 ml/½ teaspoon dried mixed herbs
>   2 cloves garlic, crushed
>   10 ml/2 teaspoons chopped parsley
>   45 g/1½ oz butter
>   45 ml/3 tablespoons plain flour
>   625 ml/1 pint milk or half milk, half Fish
>   Stock (this page)
>   125 ml/4 fl oz single cream (optional)
>   chopped parsley to garnish

Mix together the salmon, tomatoes, onion, water, pepper, mixed herbs, garlic and parsley. Microwave on High for 4–5 minutes. Cool slightly, then process until smooth.

Microwave the butter on High for 50 seconds to melt. Stir in the flour, then gradually add the milk or milk and stock, stirring continuously. Microwave on High for 5–6 minutes, stirring a few times — until the sauce thickens.

Mix the sauce with the salmon mixture and stir well. Reheat the soup on High for 2–3 minutes. Stir in the cream, if using, garnish with parsley and serve.

VARIATIONS: Substitute 440 g/14 oz canned prawns or mussels for the salmon.

FISH STOCK

Homemade stock will enhance the flavour of any fish dish and is so easy to make.

>   1 kg/2 lb white fish bones, heads and
>   trimmings
>   1 onion, chopped
>   1 leek, sliced
>   1 stick celery, sliced
>   1 carrot, peeled and diced
>   juice of ½ lemon
>   125 ml/4 fl oz dry white wine
>   6 white peppercorns
>   1 bouquet garni
>   1 litre/1¾ pints water
>   5 ml/1 teaspoon salt

Wash the fish heads and place them in a large bowl with the remaining ingredients. Cover and microwave on High for 10 minutes, then microwave on Medium-High for 20 minutes. (You can boil the stock, uncovered, on High for a more concentrated flavour, but I find that this is not necessary.) Strain and use, or pour into ice-cube trays and freeze. MAKES 1 LITRE/1¾ PINTS.

Mediterranean Fish (page 10).

Tuna Fish Cakes (page 9) served with Homemade Tomato Sauce (page 9), and Salmon Bisque (page 6).

MEDITERRANEAN FISH SOUP

2 large potatoes, peeled and cubed
45 ml/3 tablespoons water
45 ml/3 tablespoons olive oil
2 onions, chopped
2 cloves garlic, crushed
2 sticks celery, chopped
15 ml/1 tablespoon plain flour
1 litre/1¾ pints boiling water
4 tomatoes, peeled and chopped
12.5 ml/2½ teaspoons tomato paste
few drops of Tabasco
salt and freshly ground black pepper to taste
sprig of fresh thyme or basil
750 g/1½ lb fish fillets (such as haddock,
    monkfish or cod), cubed

Microwave the potatoes and 45 ml/3 tablespoons water in a bowl, covered, on High for 6 minutes; set aside.

Microwave the olive oil, onions, garlic and celery in another large bowl on High for 6 minutes, stirring after 3 minutes. Stir in the flour, then gradually add the boiling water. Microwave on High for 4 minutes, stirring once. Add the potatoes and liquid, tomatoes, tomato paste, Tabasco, seasoning and thyme or basil to the bowl, and stir. Microwave on High for 10–12 minutes, stirring a few times. Mix in the fish, cover, and microwave on High for 4–5 minutes — until the fish is cooked. Remove the sprig of thyme or basil, taste to see if more seasoning is required, and serve hot.

VARIATION: For a special occasion, add a combination of seafood (such as squid rings, prawns, mussels or clams) to the soup when you add the fish.

HAWAIIAN PILCHARDS

Serve with Yellow Rice (see page 13) and a salad.

875 g/1¾ lb canned pilchards in tomato sauce
440 g/14 oz canned pineapple chunks
30 g/1 oz butter
½ green pepper, seeded and cut into strips
½ red pepper, seeded and cut into strips
4 spring onions, chopped
chilli powder to taste
5 ml/1 teaspoon soy sauce
salt and freshly ground black pepper to taste
chopped parsley to garnish

Drain the pilchards, keeping the fish whole, and reserve the sauce. Arrange the pilchards in a dish. Drain the pineapple chunks, reserving the juice. Arrange the pineapple chunks on top of the fish.

In a glass bowl, microwave the butter, peppers, spring onions and chilli powder on High for 3–4 minutes — until soft. Mix in the sauce from the pilchards, the reserved pineapple juice, soy sauce and seasoning. Microwave on High for 3 minutes. Pour the sauce over the pilchards and pineapple chunks. Cover and microwave on High for about 8 minutes. Stand for 2–3 minutes, garnish with parsley, then serve.

TUNA FISH CAKES

Serve with Homemade Tomato sauce (this page) or Curry Sauce (page 21) and curly endive or lettuce leaves.

200 g/6½ oz canned tuna, drained and flaked
250 g/8 oz Mashed Potato (page 14)
15 ml/1 tablespoon melted butter
1 egg, lightly beaten
25 ml/5 teaspoons plain flour
salt to taste
pinch of cayenne pepper
15 ml/1 tablespoon chopped spring onion
15 ml/1 tablespoon chopped parsley
1 egg, lightly beaten, to coat
125 g/4 oz dried breadcrumbs, seasoned
15 ml/1 tablespoon oil

Mix together the tuna, potato, butter, egg, flour, salt, cayenne, spring onion and parsley. Shape the mixture into about six patties. Dip them in egg, then coat in breadcrumbs. Refrigerate for 30 minutes to set the coating.

Preheat a browning dish on High for 6 minutes. Add the oil. Place the fish cakes in the oil in the fish and press them down with a spatula. Microwave on High for 4–5 minutes, turning after 2 minutes. Drain and serve.

HOMEMADE TOMATO SAUCE

Refrigerate for up to two days, or freeze leftovers.

15 ml/1 tablespoon butter
1 small onion, chopped
5 ripe tomatoes, peeled, seeded and
   roughly chopped
10 ml/1½ teaspoons fresh lemon juice
1 clove garlic, crushed
5 ml/1 teaspoon caster sugar
5 ml/1 teaspoon dried basil
30 ml/2 tablespoons chopped parsley
sprig of fresh thyme
salt and freshly ground pepper to taste

Microwave the butter and onion in a glass bowl on High for 3 minutes. Add the remaining ingredients and microwave on High for about 5 minutes — until boiling. Stir, then microwave on Medium-High for 10–12 minutes, stirring occasionally — until thick and pulpy. Remove the thyme and liquidize. If the sauce is too thin, simmer on High until it thickens. Serve hot. If the sauce is refrigerated, reheat it on Medium-High before serving.

FISH STEW

Serve with crusty bread to mop up the juices.

30 g/1 oz butter
2 onions, chopped
2 potatoes, peeled and diced
2 carrots, peeled and sliced
750 ml/24 fl oz hot Fish Stock (page 6)
125 ml/4 fl oz dry white wine
1 bayleaf
2 tomatoes, peeled and chopped
pinch of dried thyme
2.5 ml/½ teaspoon salt
2.5 ml/½ teaspoon pepper
500 g/1 lb firm fish fillets (such as cod,
   haddock or salmon), cubed
15 ml/1 tablespoon chopped parsley
45 ml/3 tablespoons single cream (optional)

Place the butter, onions, potatoes and carrots in a bowl; microwave, covered, on High for 8–10 minutes. Add the stock, wine, bayleaf, tomatoes, thyme, salt and pepper; microwave, uncovered, on High for 5 minutes; then cover and microwave on Medium-High for 8 minutes. Check the vegetables are tender. Add the fish and microwave on Medium-High for 6–8 minutes — until it is cooked. Remove the bayleaf, sprinkle with parsley and stir in the cream, if using. Spoon into soup bowls to serve.

PAN-FRIED TROUT FILLETS

Serve with Lemon Butter Sauce (this page).

> 750 g/1½ lb trout fillets
> coarse sea salt
> 45 g/1½ oz plain flour
> freshly ground black pepper to taste
> 2 eggs, beaten
> 185 g/6 oz dried breadcrumbs, seasoned
> 155 ml/¼ pint oil
> 22 g/¾ oz butter

Sprinkle the fish generously with salt. Refrigerate for 30 minutes to firm the fish, then dust off the salt.

Mix the flour and pepper together. Dust the fish with the mixture, then dip it into the egg and coat with the breadcrumbs. Refrigerate for 30 minutes to set the crust.

Preheat a browning dish on High for 6–8 minutes, add the oil and butter, and microwave on High for 4 minutes. Add the crumbed fish fillets and microwave on High for about 7 minutes, turning after 3 minutes — until cooked. Drain and serve.

LEMON BUTTER SAUCE

> 30 g/1 oz butter
> 45 ml/3 tablespoons lemon juice
> 2.5 ml/½ teaspoon salt
> 10 ml/2 teaspoons caster sugar
> freshly ground black pepper to taste
> 5 ml/1 teaspoon paprika

Mix all the ingredients together well, then microwave on High for 2 minutes. Pour the sauce over fried or grilled fish to serve. MAKES ABOUT 75 ML/2½ FL OZ.

RICE SALAD

> 200 g/6½ oz rice
> 625 ml/1 pint boiling water
> 5 ml/1 teaspoon salt
> 100 ml/3½ fl oz French dressing
> 45 ml/3 tablespoons chopped celery
> ½ red pepper, seeded and diced
> 10 black olives, pitted and halved

Microwave the rice, water and salt, covered, on High for 10–15 minutes. Stand for 15 minutes, then stir in the remaining ingredients. Refrigerate; allow to warm to room temperature before serving.

MEDITERRANEAN FISH

This looks and tastes fantastic! Serve with French bread, to mop up the juices, and a crisp salad.

> 750 g–1 kg/1½–2 lb firm fish fillets (such
>   as cod, hake or haddock)
>
> MEDITERRANEAN SAUCE
> 1 large onion, chopped
> 1 clove garlic, crushed
> 12.5 ml/2½ teaspoons olive oil
> 410 g/13 oz canned chopped tomatoes
> 125 ml/4 fl oz dry white wine
> pinch of caster sugar
> salt and freshly ground black pepper to taste
> 12.5 ml/2½ teaspoons cornflour
> 20 ml/4 teaspoons water
> 12 black olives, pitted and halved
> 15 ml/1 tablespoon chopped parsley
> 15 ml/1 tablespoon capers

Place the fish in a large, flat-bottomed dish.

To make the sauce, microwave the onion, garlic and oil on High for 4 minutes. Add the tomatoes and liquid, wine, sugar and seasoning. Microwave on High for 10–12 minutes. Blend the cornflour and water to a smooth paste, stir into the sauce, then microwave on High for 2–3 minutes. Stir in the olives, parsley and capers. Pour the sauce over the fish and microwave on High for 11–13½ minutes (depends on how much fish you use). Stand for 4 minutes, then serve.

COMBINATION OVEN: Cook at 200 °C and medium microwave power level for 14 minutes (20–25 minutes if your oven alternates convection and microwave energy).

FISH FILLETS IN CUCUMBER SAUCE

A bowl of savoury rice and a simple salad will round off this light dish.

> 750 g/1½ lb fish fillets (such as sole or plaice)
> 410 g/13 oz canned condensed cream
>   of celery soup
> 60 g/2 oz cucumber, chopped
> 15 ml/1 tablespoon sliced spring onions
> 15 ml/1 tablespoon dry white wine
> 2.5 ml/½ teaspoon chopped dill

Roll up the fish fillets, skin-side inside, and place them in a round casserole, seam-side down. Combine the remaining ingredients and pour over the fish. Cover and microwave on High for 10–12 minutes — until cooked. Stand for about 4 minutes before serving.

Pan-Fried Trout Fillets (page 10) and Fish Fillets in Cucumber Sauce (page 10).

FISH TETRAZZINI

750 g/1½ lb hake fillets
1 bayleaf
salt and freshly ground black pepper to taste
25 ml/5 teaspoons lemon juice
200 g/6½ oz button mushrooms, sliced
30 g/1 oz butter
2 onions, chopped
1 green pepper, seeded and chopped
250 g/8 oz rindless bacon, chopped
410 g/13 oz canned mushroom soup
250 ml/8 fl oz single cream or plain yoghurt
30 ml/2 tablespoons sherry
200 g/6½ oz Cheddar cheese, grated
250 g/8 oz fusilli, cooked (see Pasta,
    page 43)
60 g/2 oz dried breadcrumbs, seasoned
5 ml/1 teaspoon paprika

Place the fish, bayleaf, seasoning and lemon juice in a flat-bottomed dish, cover, and microwave on High for 7½ minutes. Cool, then remove the bayleaf and flake the fish with a fork.

Microwave the mushrooms and butter in a small bowl on High for 3 minutes.

Mix the onions, green pepper and bacon together in a bowl, and microwave on High for 5 minutes. Stir in the mushroom soup, cooked mushrooms, cream or yoghurt, sherry and half the grated cheese. Mix in the flaked fish and fusilli, and spoon the mixture into a large casserole. Sprinkle with the remaining cheese, breadcrumbs and paprika. Microwave on Medium for about 15 minutes. Stand for about 5 minutes, then serve.

COMBINATION OVEN: Cook at 200 °C and medium-low microwave power level for 16–18 minutes (about 25 minutes if your oven alternates convection and microwave energy).

Fish Bobotie (page 13) served with Creamy Curry Sauce (page 13), Yellow Rice (page 13) and sambals.

FISH FILLETS AU GRATIN

750 g/1½ lb fish fillets (such as cod, hake
   or plaice)
juice of 1 lemon
45 ml/3 tablespoons dry white wine
1 bayleaf
30 g/1 oz butter
1 onion, chopped
1 clove garlic, crushed
1 green pepper, seeded and chopped
30 ml/2 tablespoons plain flour
250 ml/8 fl oz milk
salt and freshly ground black pepper to taste
60 g/2 oz Cheddar cheese, grated
45 g/1½ oz dried breadcrumbs, seasoned
paprika to taste
chopped parsley to garnish

Arrange the fish in a flat-bottomed dish. Pour the lemon juice and white wine over, and add the bayleaf. Cover and microwave on High for 6–7 minutes. Stand, then drain the fish, reserving the cooking juices. Remove the bayleaf. Keep the fish warm while you make the sauce.

Microwave the butter, onion, garlic and green pepper in a glass bowl on High for 4–5 minutes. Stir in the flour. Add the milk and reserved cooking juices, and stir well. Season, then microwave on High for 4 minutes, stirring after 2 minutes.

Pour the sauce over the fish and sprinkle the grated cheese, dried breadcrumbs and paprika over. Microwave on High for 3–4 minutes. Garnish with parsley and serve.

VARIATIONS
◆ Instead of the green pepper, use 100 g/3½ oz button mushrooms, sliced.
◆ Use 4 spring onions, chopped, instead of the onion.

FISH BOBOTIE

Serve with Yellow Rice (this page), Poppadums (page 24) and Creamy Curry Sauce (this page).

750 g/1½ lb hake fillets, skinned
2 slices white bread, crusts removed
125 ml/4 fl oz milk
2 onions, chopped
30 g/1 oz butter
2 cloves garlic, crushed
10 ml/2 teaspoons grated fresh ginger
15 ml/1 tablespoon curry powder
5 ml/1 teaspoon turmeric
25 ml/5 teaspoons chutney
25 ml/5 teaspoons lemon juice
10 ml/2 teaspoons grated lemon zest
salt and freshly ground black pepper to taste
5 ml/1 teaspoon caster sugar
2 eggs, beaten
125 ml/4 fl oz buttermilk
4–6 bayleaves
toasted almond flakes (optional)

Process the fish in a food processor. Soak the bread in the milk. Mix the bread and fish together.

Place the onions, butter, garlic and ginger in a glass bowl and microwave on High for 5 minutes. Stir in the curry powder and turmeric, and microwave on High for 1 minute. Add to the fish mixture with the chutney, lemon juice and zest, seasoning and sugar. Mix well, then place in a casserole. Smooth the top.

Mix the eggs and the buttermilk together and pour over the fish mixture. Press in the bayleaves, sprinkle with almond flakes, if using, and microwave on Medium-High for 20–25 minutes — until the mixture is firm and the egg topping is set. Stand for 7–8 minutes, then serve.

COMBINATION OVEN: Cook at 200 °C and medium-low microwave power level for 20–25 minutes (about 30 minutes if your oven alternates convection and micro-wave energy).

CREAMY CURRY SAUCE

30 g/1 oz butter
30 ml/2 tablespoons plain flour
5 ml/1 teaspoon curry powder
200 ml/6½ fl oz coconut milk

Microwave the butter in a glass bowl on High for 40 seconds. Stir in the flour and curry powder. Gradually stir in the coconut milk, then microwave on High for 3 minutes — until the sauce thickens. Serve hot.

SPICY FISH CURRY

This is a mild curry that is best made with firm fish. Don't overcook it as the fish cubes disintegrate and this makes the dish look messy. Serve the curry with Yellow Rice (this page) and Indian-style side dishes.

20 ml/4 teaspoons oil
750 g/1½ lb fish fillets (such as monkfish,
    cod or haddock), cubed
fish seasoning to taste
1 onion, chopped
5 ml/1 teaspoon grated fresh ginger
1 clove garlic, crushed
1 green pepper, seeded and diced
1 green chilli, seeded and diced
10–15 ml/2–3 teaspoons curry powder
125 ml/4 fl oz water
12.5 ml/2½ teaspoons cornflour (optional)
100 ml/3½ fl oz low-fat plain yoghurt
fresh coriander leaves to garnish

Preheat a browning dish on High for 6 minutes. Add the oil and microwave on High for 1 minute. Pat the cubed fish dry with a paper towel, season, and add immediately to the browning dish. Microwave on High for 3 minutes. Remove the fish and add the onion, ginger, garlic, green pepper and chilli to the browning dish. Microwave on High for 2 minutes. Stir, then mix in the curry powder. Microwave on High for 20 minutes. Mix in the fish cubes and the water. Microwave on High for about 5 minutes — until the fish is cooked. If desired, thicken the sauce with cornflour mixed into a paste with a little water. Stir in the yoghurt. Microwave on Medium-High for 2 minutes. Garnish the curry with coriander leaves and serve as suggested above.

YELLOW RICE

This colourful and tasty rice is the traditional accompaniment to curry dishes.

200 g/6½ oz rice
625 ml/1 pint boiling water
5 ml/1 teaspoon salt
5 ml/1 teaspoon turmeric
1 stick cinnamon
60 g/2 oz raisins

Place all the ingredients in a large bowl and microwave, covered, on High for 10–15 minutes. Stand for about 15 minutes, remove the cinnamon stick, then fluff up the rice with a fork and serve.

To reheat, microwave the rice, covered, on High for 3–5 minutes.

BAKED FISH IN ORANGE SAUCE

A colourful and tasty dish. Citrus Rice (this page) and a simple green salad are ideal accompaniments.

750 g/1½ lb fish fillets (such as cod,
    salmon or halibut)
juice of 1 orange
12.5 ml/2½ teaspoons Drambuie
5 ml/1 teaspoon white wine vinegar
5 ml/1 teaspoon caster sugar
30 g/1 oz butter, melted
5 ml/1 teaspoon grated orange zest
salt and freshly ground black pepper to taste
pinch of freshly grated nutmeg
5 ml/1 teaspoon cornflour
fresh watercress and slices of fresh orange
    to garnish

Place the fish fillets in a flat-bottomed dish. Mix together the orange juice, Drambuie, vinegar, sugar, butter, orange zest and seasoning, and pour over the fish. Sprinkle with the nutmeg, then microwave on High for 8–10 minutes — until the fish is cooked. Transfer the fish to a serving dish.

To thicken the sauce, mix the cornflour to a paste with a little water and stir in. Microwave on High for 2 minutes. Spoon the sauce over the fish. Garnish with watercress and orange, then serve.

VARIATION: Any orange-flavoured liqueur can be used instead of the Drambuie.

CITRUS RICE

1 onion, finely chopped
45 g/1½ oz butter
200 g/6½ oz rice
315 ml/½ pint fresh orange juice
315 ml/½ pint boiling water
2.5 ml/½ teaspoon turmeric
5 ml/1 teaspoon grated orange zest
5 ml/1 teaspoon salt
good pinch of dried thyme
fresh watercress to garnish

In a deep glass bowl, microwave the onion and butter on High for 3 minutes. Add the rice, stir, then microwave on High for 2–3 minutes — until the butter is absorbed. Add the orange juice, boiling water, turmeric, orange zest, salt and thyme. Stir well, then cover the bowl and microwave on High for 12–15 minutes. Stand for about 5 minutes, then fluff up the rice with a fork, garnish with watercress, and serve hot with fish dishes.

COLD BAKED FISH WITH THICK AVOCADO SAUCE

A lovely cold dish to serve in summer accompanied by Rice Salad (page 10) or a colourful salad of crisp lettuce leaves, tomato wedges, onion rings, cucumber slices and quartered hard-boiled eggs, tossed with an oil and vinegar dressing.

750 g/1½ lb firm fish fillets (such as cod
    or salmon)
freshly ground black pepper to taste
pinch of dried dill
fish seasoning to taste
125 ml/4 fl oz dry white wine

AVOCADO SAUCE
1 large, ripe avocado
salt and freshly ground black pepper to taste
100 ml/3½ fl oz pineapple-flavoured yoghurt
2 slices fresh pineapple, grated
dash of lemon juice

fresh pineapple slices and snipped chives
    to garnish

Place the fish fillets in a flat-bottomed dish, season with pepper, dill and fish seasoning and pour the white wine over. Microwave, covered, on High for 7–8 minutes — until the fish is cooked. Cool the fish in the liquid, then remove it from the dish and place it on a bed of lettuce leaves on a serving plate.

To make the sauce, mash the flesh of the avocado, season, then mix in the yoghurt, grated pineapple and lemon juice. Spoon dollops of the avocado mixture on to the fish. Garnish the dish with sliced pineapple and a sprinkling of snipped chives.

VARIATION: Refrigerate the sauce until firm, then pipe it on to the fish in spirals or patterns with a piping bag.

MASHED POTATO

6 medium potatoes, peeled and cubed
155 ml/¼ pint boiling water
45 ml/3 tablespoons milk
15 ml/1 tablespoon butter

Microwave the potatoes and water in a bowl, covered, on High for 8–10 minutes — until the potatoes are soft. Stand for about 3 minutes, drain, then mash. Add the milk and butter, and mix in well. MAKES ABOUT 500 G/1 LB.

VARIATION: Add 30 ml/2 tablespoons fresh snipped chives and use soured cream instead of the milk.

Baked Fish in Orange Sauce (page 14) and Cold Baked Fish with Thick Avocado Sauce (page 14).

FISHERMAN'S PIE

It will take a little time to put this dish together but the effort will be rewarded by everyone's enjoyment of it. Use leftover Mashed Potato (page 14) to save time.

750 g/1½ lb hake
500 ml/16 fl oz milk
2 onions, sliced
4 peppercorns
2 bayleaves
salt and freshly ground black pepper to taste

SAUCE
30 g/1 oz butter
125 g/4 oz button mushrooms, quartered
30 ml/2 tablespoons plain flour
30 ml/2 tablespoons single cream
2 hard-boiled eggs, chopped
30 ml/2 tablespoons chopped parsley

TOPPING
500 g/1 lb Mashed Potato (page 14)
1 egg, separated
paprika to taste

Place the hake, milk, onions, peppercorns, bayleaves and seasoning in a dish, and microwave, covered, on High for 8–10 minutes. Remove the fish and flake it. Strain the liquid and reserve it for the sauce.

To make the sauce, microwave the butter and mushrooms in a bowl on High for about 3 minutes. Stir in the flour and microwave on High for 30 seconds. Add the reserved liquid and microwave on High for 2 minutes — until thickened. Stir in the cream, chopped eggs and parsley, then mix in the flaked fish. Spoon the mixture into a pie dish.

Mix the potato with the egg yolk. Whisk the egg white until stiff and fold in. Spoon the potato over the fish mixture and sprinkle with paprika. Microwave on High for about 12 minutes — until the top is browned. Stand for about 4 minutes before serving.

COMBINATION OVEN: Cook at 200 °C and medium-low microwave power level for 12–15 minutes (25–30 minutes if your oven alternates convection and microwave energy).

VARIATIONS: Turn this into a very special dish by substituting 250 g/8 oz shrimps or mussels for 250 g/8 oz of the hake and adding to the sauce with the cream.

Mediterranean Mussels (page 17) and Asparagus and Oyster Bake (page 17).

FISH LOAF WITH CRUNCHY COATING

Slices of this easy fish loaf can be served warm or cold with Cold Soured Cream Sauce (this page). Homemade Tomato Sauce (page 9) is also a good accompaniment.

> 30 ml/2 tablespoons fresh brown breadcrumbs
> 750 g/1½ lb hake, minced
> 15 ml/1 tablespoon chopped parsley
> 1 onion, grated
> 1 piece pimiento, chopped
> 5 ml/1 teaspoon salt
> pinch of cayenne pepper
> freshly ground white pepper to taste
> 2 eggs, lightly beaten
> 125 ml/4 fl oz milk
> fennel or curly endive leaves to garnish

Grease a big ring mould or loaf pan. Sprinkle lightly with half the brown breadcrumbs. Mix the hake, parsley, onion, pimiento, salt, cayenne and white pepper, eggs and milk together, and pack the mixture into the ring mould or loaf pan. Sprinkle the top with the remaining breadcrumbs. Microwave on Medium-High for 8–10 minutes. Garnish with fennel or endive leaves, and serve warm, or refrigerate if serving cold.

COLD SOURED CREAM SAUCE

This sauce is also good with cold chicken.

> 250 ml/8 fl oz soured cream
> 25 ml/5 teaspoons lemon juice or vinegar
> 5 ml/1 teaspoon salt
> 5 ml/1 teaspoon Worcestershire sauce
> 2.5 ml/½ teaspoon mustard powder
> 15 ml/1 tablespoon grated onion
> 25 ml/5 teaspoons chopped parsley
> pinch of cayenne pepper

Mix all the ingredients together well. Refrigerate the sauce until needed. MAKES ABOUT 315 ML/½ PINT.

CHILLED SEAFOOD CURRY

440 g/14 oz firm fish fillets, cubed
10 ml/2 teaspoons lemon juice
pinch of dried dill
salt and freshly ground black pepper to taste
155 g/5 oz peeled prawns (see Notes,
    page 6)
1 red pepper, seeded and cut into long strips
1 avocado, peeled and cubed
juice of 1 lemon

CURRY SAUCE
60 ml/4 tablespoons plain yoghurt
45 ml/3 tablespoons mayonnaise
10 ml/2 teaspoons curry powder
1 clove garlic, crushed
salt and freshly ground black pepper to taste

chopped fresh dill or coriander to garnish

Place the fish in a flat-bottomed dish and sprinkle with the lemon juice, dill and seasoning. Microwave on High for 4 minutes, then drain and refrigerate until firm.

Mix the fish with the prawns. Add the pepper. Coat the avocado with the lemon juice, then add to the fish, reserving the lemon juice. Cover the mixture and place it in the refrigerator to chill.

Mix all the ingredients for the sauce together. Thin down with a little of the reserved lemon juice, then spoon the sauce over the chilled fish mixture. Garnish with chopped fresh herbs and serve.

ASPARAGUS AND OYSTER FISH BAKE

Great for a special occasion! Serve with Rice (page 21).

750 g/1½ lb firm fish fillets
410 g/13 oz canned asparagus spears
1 onion, chopped
salt and freshly ground black pepper to taste
5 ml/1 teaspoon dried thyme
100 ml/3½ fl oz dry white wine
100 g/3½ oz canned smoked oysters

CREAMY SAUCE
45 g/1½ oz butter
45 ml/3 tablespoons plain flour
125 ml/4 fl oz Fish Stock (page 6)
milk
2 egg yolks, beaten
15 ml/1 tablespoon lemon juice
125 ml/4 fl oz single cream
15 ml/1 tablespoon chopped parsley

Place the fish in a casserole. Drain the can of asparagus spears, reserving the liquid, and layer the asparagus over the fish. Sprinkle the onion, seasoning and thyme on top. Pour the wine over and top with the oysters.

To make the sauce, microwave the butter in a bowl on High for 50 seconds. Stir in the flour, then the stock. Add milk to the asparagus liquid to make up to 155 ml/¼ pint; add to the sauce. Microwave on High for 4 minutes, stirring after 2 minutes. Stir. Blend the egg yolks, lemon juice, cream and parsley; stir into the sauce. Microwave on Medium for 2–3 minutes. Pour the sauce over the fish. Microwave on Medium for 10–12 minutes — until the fish is cooked. Stand for 4 minutes, then serve.

COMBINATION OVEN: Cook at 200 °C and medium microwave power level for 12–14 minutes (20–25 minutes if your oven alternates convection and microwave energy).

MEDITERRANEAN MUSSELS

Dip slices of crusty bread into the delicious sauce and serve the mussels with a bowl of Rice Salad (page 10) and a crisp green salad on the side.

12.5 ml/2½ teaspoons olive oil
1 onion, chopped
2 cloves garlic, crushed
1 bayleaf
2.5 ml/½ teaspoon dried mixed herbs
4 large tomatoes, peeled, seeded and chopped
salt and freshly ground black pepper to taste
pinch of caster sugar
45 g/1½ oz black olives, pitted and quartered
250 g/8 oz rindless streaky bacon
2 kg/4 lb mussels, scrubbed and beards removed
125 ml/4 fl oz dry white wine
45 ml/3 tablespoons chopped parsley

Microwave the oil, onion, garlic, bayleaf and mixed herbs, tomatoes, seasoning and sugar in a bowl on High for 8 minutes, stirring after 4 minutes. Stir in the olives, set aside and cover to keep warm.

Microwave the bacon on a rack, covered with a paper towel, on High for 30 seconds per rasher. Remove the paper towel immediately. Cool and crumble the bacon.

Place half the mussels and the wine in a casserole, and microwave, covered, on High power for 5 minutes, stirring after 2½ minutes. Microwave the remaining mussels in the liquid in the casserole on High for 5 minutes, stirring after 2½ minutes. Discard any mussels with unopened shells.

Place the cooked mussels on a serving platter. Pour the tomato sauce over, top with bacon and parsley, and serve.

CHAPTER TWO

Meat

MEAT, a great source of protein, is more affordable if cooked in a microwave. The traditional Sunday roast not only cooks in a third of the time that conventional cooking takes but there is less shrinkage and the meat won't overcook or dry out.

NOTES
◆ Always buy the best quality meat because, unlike conventional cooking, the microwave will not tenderize a poor quality grade of meat.
◆ Always defrost meat before cooking. Cover when defrosting and turn over once to ensure even defrosting. Where possible, allow meat to stand, equal to the time it took to defrost.
◆ Never salt meat before or during cooking.

BEEF AND VEGETABLE SOUP

Serve this hearty soup with Spicy Croûtons (this page).

750 g/1½ lb beef shin, cut into small cubes
410 ml/13 fl oz water
1 onion, chopped
3 carrots, peeled and sliced
2 turnips, peeled and chopped
4 sticks celery, sliced
15 ml/1 tablespoon butter
1.5 litres/2¾ pints hot beef stock
500 g/1 lb tomatoes, peeled and chopped
12.5 ml/2½ teaspoons Worcestershire sauce

Place the beef and water in a casserole and microwave on High for 6–8 minutes — until boiling, then microwave on Medium for 35–40 minutes — until the meat is tender. Place the vegetables in a dish with the butter and microwave, covered, on High for 10–12 minutes, stirring after 5 minutes — until the vegetables are soft. Add the vegetables to the beef with the stock, tomatoes and Worcestershire sauce. Microwave on High for 12–15 minutes, then on Medium for 15 minutes. Serve hot.

NOTE: Soup improves in flavour if made in advance and then reheated on High before serving.

SPICY CROUTONS

20 ml/4 teaspoons oil
3 slices bread, crusts removed
2.5 ml/½ teaspoon paprika

Preheat a browning dish on High for 8 minutes. Add the oil. Cube the bread. Sprinkle with paprika and add to the oil in the browning dish. Microwave on High for 1½ minutes. Turn, and microwave on High for 1 minute. Drain. Add to soup just before serving.

VARIATION: Add 1 clove garlic, crushed, to the oil when you add the bread.

WINTER SALAD

½ head of cabbage, shredded
100 g/3½ oz cheese of your choice, cubed
30 ml/2 tablespoons pine nuts
1 stick celery, sliced
1 small onion, chopped
1 apple, cored and chopped

DRESSING
5 ml/1 teaspoon clear honey
2.5 ml/½ teaspoon mustard powder
30 ml/2 tablespoons plain yoghurt
45 ml/3 tablespoons sunflower oil
10 ml/2 teaspoons lemon juice
pinch of celery salt

snipped fresh chives to garnish

Mix the salad ingredients together. Microwave the honey in a bowl on High for 10 seconds, add to the rest of the ingredients for the dressing, blend well and pour over the salad. Garnish with chives.

Beef and Vegetable Soup (page 18) and Winter Salad (page 18).

19

Chinese Beef Ring (page 21) served with Rice (page 21).

BOBOTIE

30 g/1 oz butter
1 onion, chopped
1 thick slice bread
100 ml/3½ fl oz milk
750 g/1½ lb minced beef
15 ml/1 tablespoon smooth apricot jam
30 ml/2 tablespoons lemon juice
45 g/1½ oz raisins
30 g/1 oz slivered almonds
25 ml/5 teaspoons curry powder
5 ml/1 teaspoon turmeric
25 ml/5 teaspoons chutney
salt and freshly ground black pepper to taste
4 bayleaves
2 eggs
155 ml/¼ pint buttermilk

Microwave the butter and onion in a large casserole on High for 3–4 minutes. Soak the bread in the milk, then add to the onion. Add the mince, apricot jam, lemon juice, raisins, almonds, curry powder, turmeric and chutney. Mix thoroughly and season. Cover and microwave on High for 10 minutes, stirring once during cooking. Stir well, smooth the top, and push in the bayleaves. Beat the eggs with the buttermilk and pour the mixture over the meat. Microwave, uncovered, on Medium-High for 10–12 minutes — until the top has set. Stand for 3–4 minutes before serving.

COMBINATION OVEN: Cook at 200 °C and medium-low microwave power level for 12–14 minutes (25–30 minutes if your oven alternates convection and microwave energy).

VARIATION: Sprinkle toasted almonds on top, then serve.

CURRY MEAT LOAF

A spicy meat loaf. Serve it sliced with a jug of Curry Sauce (this page), a bowl of Yellow Rice (page 13) and a tossed green salad.

1 thick slice white bread
155 ml/¼ pint milk
1 Granny Smith apple, peeled, cored and roughly chopped
1 onion, chopped
15 ml/1 tablespoon curry powder
5 ml/1 teaspoon salt
1 banana, thinly sliced
25 ml/5 teaspoons desiccated coconut
25 ml/5 teaspoons sultanas
12.5 ml/2½ teaspoons soft brown sugar
750 g/1½ lb lean minced beef
45 ml/3 tablespoons tomato ketchup
45 ml/3 tablespoons chutney

Soak the bread in the milk for 10 minutes, then squeeze to remove excess liquid. Mix the bread lightly with the remaining ingredients (do not overmix the ingredients). Pile into a greased 1-kg/2-lb loaf pan. Microwave on Medium-High for 15–18 minutes. Cover and stand for 5–6 minutes, then slice and serve.

CURRY SAUCE

This spicy, creamy sauce is also excellent with Bobotie (page 20). Serve it warm.

315 ml/½ pint milk, warmed
½ onion, chopped
freshly grated nutmeg to taste
1 bayleaf
5 peppercorns
salt and freshly ground black pepper to taste
30 g/1 oz butter
1 small onion, chopped
10 ml/2 teaspoons curry powder
30 ml/2 tablespoons plain flour
45 ml/3 tablespoons soured cream

Mix the milk with the ½ onion, nutmeg, bayleaf, pepper-corns and seasoning, and leave to infuse. Meanwhile, microwave the butter and small onion in a glass bowl (the curry will stain plastic) on High for 3 minutes. Stir in the curry powder. Microwave on High for 1 minute. Stir in the flour. Strain the milk and gradually add to the curry mixture, stirring well. Microwave on High for 2 minutes. Stir, then microwave on High for another 2 minutes. Stir in the soured cream and serve while still warm.

CHINESE BEEF RING

Serve with Rice (this page) or noodles (see Pasta, page 43).

1 onion, chopped
15 ml/1 tablespoon butter
10 ml/2 teaspoons soy sauce
12.5/2½ teaspoons dry sherry
750 g/1½ lb minced beef
45 g/1½ oz fresh breadcrumbs
5 ml/1 teaspoon Worcestershire sauce

SWEET AND SOUR SAUCE
12.5 ml/2½ teaspoons oil
1 small onion, cut into rings
1 green pepper, seeded and cut into thin strips
2 carrots, peeled and cut in julienne strips
410 g/13 oz canned pineapple chunks
12.5 ml/2½ teaspoons white wine vinegar
12.5/2½ teaspoons soft brown sugar
15 ml/1 tablespoon cornflour
2.5 ml/½ teaspoon ground ginger

In a bowl, microwave the onion and butter on High for 3 minutes. Mix lightly with the remaining ingredients for the beef ring and press the mixture into a lightly greased ring mould. Microwave on Medium-High for about 20 minutes — until the beef ring is firmly cooked. Stand for 4–5 minutes, then drain off the juices. Make the sauce while the beef ring is standing.

To make the sauce, microwave the oil, onion and green pepper on High for 3 minutes. Add the carrots, cover and microwave on High for 5 minutes. Add the pineapple chunks and juice, vinegar, sugar, cornflour and ginger, and stir in. Microwave on High for 3–4 minutes — until the sauce thickens.

To serve, unmould the ring on to a serving plate, pile rice or noodles in the centre and pour the sauce over and around the beef ring.

VARIATION: Use a mixture of vegetables of your choice for the sauce.

RICE

Cook pearl wheat in the same way as rice.

200 g/6½ oz rice
625 ml/1 pint boiling water
5 ml/1 teaspoon salt

Place all the ingredients in a bowl and cover. Microwave on High for 12 minutes. Stand for 15 minutes, then fluff up with a fork and serve.

BASIC STEW

Increase the stock to 500 ml (16 fl oz) if you are going to serve this wholesome stew with Dumplings (this page).

750 g/1½ lb stewing lamb or beef, cubed
15 ml/1 tablespoon oil
1 onion, chopped
5 ml/1 teaspoon dried mixed herbs
freshly ground black pepper to taste
20 ml/4 teaspoons plain flour
250 ml/8 fl oz hot beef stock

Preheat a browning dish on High for 8 minutes. Pat the meat dry with a paper towel. Add the oil to the browning dish and microwave on High for 1 minute, then add the meat and onion. Microwave on High for 4 minutes, stirring after 2 minutes. Stir in the herbs, pepper and flour, then slowly add the stock. Cover and microwave on Medium-Low for 50 minutes, stirring after 25 minutes — until the meat is tender. Stand for 10 minutes before serving with dumplings or potatoes.

VARIATIONS
◆ TOMATO STEW: Add 410 g/13 oz tomatoes, peeled and chopped, 6 black peppercorns, 5 ml/1 teaspoon soft brown sugar and 2.5 ml/½ teaspoon dried basil 15 minutes before the end of cooking time.
◆ GREEN BEAN STEW: Add 410 g/13 oz green beans, shredded, 1 tomato, peeled and chopped, and 200 g/6½ oz potatoes, peeled and cubed, 15 minutes before the end of cooking time.
◆ BEEF STROGANOFF: Use beef. Add 250 g/8 oz mushrooms, sliced, 30 ml/2 tablespoons lemon juice, 5 ml/1 teaspoon paprika and 15 ml/1 tablespoon chopped parsley 15 minutes before the end of cooking time. Stir in 125 ml/4 fl oz soured cream just before serving.

DUMPLINGS

185 g/6 oz plain flour
7.5 ml/1½ teaspoons baking powder
pinch of salt
75 g/2½ oz butter
1 egg, beaten
155 ml/¼ pint milk
paprika to taste

Sift the dry ingredients together, and rub in the butter until the mixture looks like fine breadcrumbs. Mix the egg and milk together, and gradually add to the flour mixture. Mix to a soft dough, then divide into dumplings, each about the size of a golf ball. Spoon the dumplings on top of the stew 15 minutes before the end of cooking time and sprinkle with paprika.

MEATBALLS IN CURRIED FRUIT SAUCE

1 thick slice bread
250 ml/8 fl oz water
500 g/1 lb lean minced beef
1 egg
good pinch of freshly grated nutmeg
pinch of ground cloves
5 ml/1 teaspoon salt
pepper to taste

FRUITY CURRY SAUCE
15 ml/1 tablespoon butter
1 onion, finely chopped
15 ml/1 tablespoon curry powder
315 ml/½ pint water
2 bananas, sliced
2 cooking apples, peeled, cored and grated
12.5 ml/2½ teaspoons soft brown sugar
12.5 ml/2½ teaspoons plain flour
30 ml/2 tablespoons apricot jam
30 ml/2 tablespoons wine vinegar
5 ml/1 teaspoon salt

Soak the bread in the water. Mix the remaining ingredients for the meatballs lightly together. Squeeze the water from the bread and add the bread to the meat mixture. Form into balls and place them in a casserole.

For the sauce, microwave the butter and onion in a glass bowl on High for 3 minutes. Stir in the curry powder, then the remaining ingredients. Microwave on High for 4 minutes. Pour the sauce over the meatballs. Microwave, covered, on Medium-High for about 15 minutes. Stand for 5 minutes, then serve.

QUICK BOLOGNESE SAUCE

2 rashers rindless bacon, chopped
1 onion, chopped
1 carrot, peeled and grated
1 stick celery, chopped
410 g/13 oz lean minced beef
25 ml/5 teaspoons plain flour
315 ml/½ pint hot beef stock
440 g/14 oz canned chopped tomatoes
salt and freshly ground black pepper to taste

Microwave the bacon and vegetables on High for 4–5 minutes. Stir in the mince and break up with a fork. Microwave on High for 4–5 minutes, breaking up the mince with a fork after 2 minutes. Stir in the flour, gradually add the stock, then the tomatoes with their liquid. Season; microwave, covered, on High for 20–25 minutes. Stand for 7–8 minutes before serving.

Meatballs in Curried Fruit Sauce (page 22), and Basic Stew (page 22) served with Dumplings (page 22).

MEATBALL CASSEROLE

Serve with a mixed salad.

15 ml/1 tablespoon oil
1 onion, chopped
500 g/1 lb lean minced beef
2.5 ml/½ teaspoon cayenne pepper
30 g/1 oz fresh white breadcrumbs
1 egg
2.5 ml/½ teaspoon dried mixed herbs
salt and freshly ground black pepper to taste
155 g/5 oz rice
410 g/13 oz canned chopped tomatoes
345 ml/11 fl oz hot beef stock
5 ml/1 teaspoon Worcestershire sauce
chopped parsley to garnish

Place the oil and chopped onion in a glass bowl and microwave on High for 3 minutes. Combine the minced beef, cayenne pepper, breadcrumbs, egg, mixed herbs and seasoning, and add the cooked onion. Form the mixture into small meatballs and roll them in the rice. Arrange the meatballs in a deep casserole.

Combine the chopped tomatoes and their liquid, beef stock and Worcestershire sauce, and pour the mixture over the meatballs. Add any remaining rice to the dish, cover, and microwave on Medium-High for 20–25 minutes. Stand for 7–8 minutes, then garnish with chopped parsley before serving as suggested.

COMBINATION OVEN: Cook at 200 °C and medium-low microwave power level for 25–30 minutes (35–40 minutes if your oven alternates between convection and microwave energy).

BEEF CURRY

Serve with Poppadums (this page), a traditional accompaniment to curry.

30 ml/2 tablespoons oil
2 onions, sliced
625 g/1¼ lb stewing beef
2 cooking apples, peeled, cored and diced
15–20 ml/3–4 teaspoons curry powder
2 cloves garlic, crushed
5 ml/1 teaspoon ground cinnamon
5 ml/1 teaspoon salt
45 ml/3 tablespoons chutney
15 ml/1 tablespoon wine vinegar
10 ml/2 teaspoons soft brown sugar
100 ml/3½ fl oz tomato purée (passata)
200 ml/6½ fl oz hot beef stock
1 bayleaf
30 g/1 oz desiccated coconut
45 ml/3 tablespoons sultanas
125 ml/4 fl oz plain yoghurt (optional)

Preheat a browning dish on High for 8 minutes. Add the oil and microwave on High for 1 minute. Add the onions and meat, and microwave on High for 4 minutes, stirring after 2 minutes. Add the apples, then stir in the curry powder, garlic and cinnamon. Microwave on High for 6 minutes. Stir in the remaining ingredients, except the sultanas and yoghurt, and place in a casserole. Microwave, covered, on Medium-Low for 50 minutes. (If you wish to thicken the curry, stir in a little flour mixed to a paste with water, then microwave on Medium-Low for 3–4 minutes.) Stand for 10 minutes, then stir in the sultanas and yoghurt, if using, and serve.

COMBINATION OVEN: Cook at 160 °C and medium-low microwave power level for 50–60 minutes (about 90 minutes if your oven alternates convection and microwave energy).

VARIATION: Add vegetables (such as peeled and diced potatoes and carrots) to the curry. Microwave the vegetables, covered, in a little water on High for about 6 minutes. Add to the curry halfway through cooking time.

POPPADUMS

Prepare crispy poppadums in the microwave!

Cook two poppadums at a time. Brush them lightly with oil on each side, then place them on a paper towel on the turntable and microwave on High for 1½–2 minutes — until they puff up. They will crisp as they cool.

VEGETABLE PLATTER

The perfect vegetable dish to serve when entertaining.

Cook small quantities of a wide variety of vegetables in advance and arrange them on a serving dish. (Either use a selection of whole baby vegetables or chop vegetables into uniform-sized pieces.) Cover with pierced cling film, then, just before serving, reheat on Medium-High until piping hot. Garnish with sprigs of fresh herbs, warm a little salad dressing in the microwave and pour the dressing over the vegetables.

BURGUNDY BEEF

Serve with Rice (page 21), a tomato salad and broccoli with cheese sauce for a hearty meal.

750 g/1½ lb stewing steak, cubed
1 onion, chopped
1 clove garlic, crushed
25 ml/5 teaspoons plain flour
2.5 ml/½ teaspoon dried thyme
freshly ground black pepper to taste
100 ml/3½ fl oz red wine
155 ml/¼ pint hot beef stock
12.5 ml/2½ teaspoons tomato paste
250 g/8 oz rindless bacon rashers, chopped
155 g/5 oz button mushrooms, sliced

Pat the meat dry. Preheat a browning dish on High for 8 minutes. Add the meat, onion and garlic to the dish, and microwave on High for 4 minutes, stirring after 2 minutes. Stir in the flour, thyme and pepper. Gradually stir in the red wine, beef stock and tomato paste. Cover and microwave on Medium-Low for 20 minutes. Add the bacon and mushrooms, and mix in well. Microwave on Medium-Low for 20–30 minutes — until the meat is tender. Stand for about 10 minutes before serving.

COMBINATION OVEN: Cook at 160 °C and medium-low microwave power level for 45–50 minutes (60–70 minutes if your oven alternates convection and microwave energy).

HINT
Always cook the food that takes the longest time first as it will also have a longer standing time and it can be covered to keep warm. So, when you are preparing a roast dinner, cook the rice first. Par-cook the potatoes and then roast them with the meat. Make the gravy and vegetables while the meat is standing.

ROAST FILLET OF BEEF

The delicious wine marinade and mushroom sauce makes this roast really special. Serve with Roast Potatoes (page 27) and Vegetable Platter (page 24). See Hint, page 24.

1.25 kg/2½ lb fillet of beef
250 ml/8 fl oz red wine
5 ml/1 teaspoon garlic salt
freshly ground black pepper to taste
5 ml/1 teaspoon mustard powder
12.5 ml/2½ teaspoons oil

MUSHROOM SAUCE
1 onion, chopped
30 g/1 oz butter
100 g/3½ chestnut mushrooms, sliced
25 ml/5 teaspoons plain flour
200 ml/6½ fl oz hot beef stock

Marinate the fillet in the wine for 24 hours in the refrigerator. Turn a few times.

Remove the meat from the marinade and dry well. Reserve the wine for the sauce. Mix the garlic salt, pepper and mustard together, and rub into the meat. Preheat a browning dish on High for 8 minutes. Add the oil, then the meat. Microwave on High for 1 minute on each side, then on Medium-High for 10 minutes on each side. Turn again and microwave on Medium-High for 8 minutes. Remove the meat from the dish and leave it to stand, covered, for 12 minutes before carving.

To make the sauce, wipe out the browning dish and add the onion and butter. Microwave on High for 2 minutes. Add the mushrooms and microwave on High for 2 minutes. Stir in the flour, then gradually stir in 155 ml/¼ pint of the reserved red wine and the stock. Microwave on High for 3–4 minutes, stirring once, then pour the sauce into a jug to serve.

COMBINATION OVEN: After browning the meat in the browning dish on High for 1 minute on each side, cook at 230 °C and medium-low microwave power level for 28 minutes (35–40 minutes if your oven alternates convection and microwave energy).

Vegetable Platter (page 24), and Roast Fillet of Beef (this page) served with Roast Potatoes (page 27).

Orange Pot Roast (page 27), and Mustard and Herb Roast Beef (this page) served with Creamed Horseradish Sauce (page 27).

MUSTARD AND HERB ROAST BEEF

Make gravy with the cooking juices. Serve with Creamed Horseradish Sauce (page 27). See Hint, page 24.

1.5 kg/3 lb entrecôte or sirloin of beef
25 ml/5 teaspoons mustard powder
20 ml/4 teaspoons oil
10 ml/2 teaspoons dried marjoram
15 ml/1 tablespoon lemon juice
2 cloves garlic, crushed
freshly ground black pepper to taste
salt to taste

GRAVY
30 g/1 oz butter
25 ml/5 teaspoons gravy powder
salt and freshly ground black pepper to taste
about 200 ml/6½ fl oz water

Pat the beef dry. Combine the mustard, oil, marjoram, lemon juice, garlic and pepper; rub into the beef. Preheat a browning dish on High for 8 minutes. Add the meat and microwave on High for 1 minute per side, then microwave on Medium-High for 24–30 minutes (8–10 minutes per 500 g/1 lb), turning after about 12 minutes. Remove the meat, reserving the juices, cover, and stand for 12–15 minutes. Add salt and slice thinly to serve.

To make the gravy, microwave the butter in a jug on High for 30 seconds. Stir in the gravy powder, seasoning, 125 ml/4 fl oz of the reserved juices and the water. Microwave on High for 3–4 minutes, stirring twice. Pour into a jug to serve.

COMBINATION OVEN: Place the meat on a greased rack and cook at 230 °C and medium microwave power level for 24–30 minutes [8–10 minutes per 500 g/1 lb] (36–42 minutes [12–14 minutes per 500 g/1 lb] if your oven alternates convection and microwave energy).

CREAMED HORSERADISH SAUCE

Roast beef is traditionally served with this distinctive sauce.

>   30 g/1 oz butter
>   25 ml/5 teaspoons plain flour
>   250 ml/8 fl oz milk
>   2.5 ml/½ teaspoon salt
>   30 ml/2 tablespoons prepared horseradish
>   25 ml/5 teaspoons double cream
>   5 ml/1 teaspoon caster sugar
>   5 ml/1 teaspoon mustard powder
>   12.5 ml/2½ teaspoons vinegar

Microwave the butter in a bowl on High for 30 seconds. Stir in the flour, gradually blend in the milk, then microwave on High for 4 minutes, stirring after 2 minutes. Add the remaining ingredients, mix well, and microwave on Medium-Low for 1 minute. Serve immediately with roast beef.

ORANGE POT ROAST

Citrus Rice (page 14) and Sweet Potatoes (this page) are the perfect accompaniments. See Hint, page 24.

>   1.5 kg/3 lb rolled topside of beef
>   100 ml/3½ fl oz fresh orange juice
>   45 ml/3 tablespoons chutney
>   5 ml/1 teaspoon grated orange zest
>   100 ml/3½ fl oz dry white wine
>   salt and freshly ground black pepper to taste
>   2.5 ml/½ teaspoon dried thyme
>   200 g/6½ oz mushrooms, sliced
>   1 onion, chopped
>   60 ml/4 tablespoons cold water
>   12.5 ml/2½ teaspoons cornflour
>   10 ml/2 teaspoons soft brown sugar

Place the meat in a large round dish with a lid. Combine the orange juice, chutney, zest, wine, seasoning and thyme in a jug. Pour the mixture over the meat. Add the mushrooms and onion, cover, and microwave on Medium-Low for about 60 minutes — until tender. Transfer the meat to a serving dish, cover and stand for about 20 minutes. Cut thin slices across the grain to serve.

To make the gravy, mix the water, cornflour and sugar together, and stir into the cooking juices in the dish. Microwave on High for 3–4 minutes — until thickened. Pour into a serving jug and cover to keep warm.

COMBINATION OVEN: Cook at 160 °C and medium-low microwave power level for 1–1¼ hours (1–1½ hours if your oven alternates convection and microwave energy).

ROAST POTATOES

The traditional accompaniment to a roast.

Peel and halve 4 medium potatoes. Microwave in a little cold water on High for about 5 minutes to par-cook. Drain and add to the roast in the browning dish 10 minutes before the end of cooking time. Turn after 5 minutes. For a combination oven, par-cook and drain, then brush with oil and place on a cooking rack with the roast at the beginning of the cooking process. Baste often with oil so that the potatoes brown.

BRISKET WITH BARBECUE SAUCE

>   1 kg/2 lb boned brisket
>   2 onions, sliced
>   freshly ground black pepper to taste
>   5 ml/1 teaspoon dried mixed herbs
>   250 ml/8 fl oz pineapple and juice
>
>   BARBECUE SAUCE
>   250 ml/8 fl oz tomato sauce
>   25 ml/5 teaspoons Worcestershire sauce
>   2.5 ml/½ teaspoon paprika
>   salt and freshly ground black pepper to taste
>   125 ml/4 fl oz mayonnaise
>   30 ml/2 tablespoons vinegar
>   pinch of cayenne pepper
>   100 g/3½ oz soft brown sugar

Place the meat in a large casserole (or oven cooking bag). Sprinkle with the onions, pepper and herbs, and pour the fruit juice over. Cover and microwave on Medium-Low for 30 minutes (15 minutes per 500 g/1 lb), turning meat every 10 minutes. Remove meat from dish (reserving juices) and allow to cool while you make the sauce.

Place the onion and cooking juices in a blender with all the ingredients for the sauce, and blend until smooth.

Slice the meat and arrange on a serving dish. Pour the sauce over. Microwave on Medium-Low for 20 minutes. Stand for about 6 minutes, then serve.

SWEET POTATOES

Serve instead of the usual roast potatoes.

Scrub, wash and pierce the skins of 750 g/1½ lb red-skinned sweet potatoes. Arrange on the turntable, microwave on High for 5 minutes, turn over; microwave on High for another 5–8 minutes, until soft. Stand for about 10 minutes, then peel and slice into rounds to serve.

CARBONNADE OF BEEF

*A delicious casserole to serve with Savoury Rice (page 39)
and Vegetable Platter (page 24).*

10 ml/2 teaspoons oil
10 ml/2 teaspoons butter
750 g/1½ lb stewing beef, cubed
75 g/2½ oz bacon, chopped
1 onion, chopped
1 clove garlic, crushed
125 ml/4 fl oz hot beef stock
250 ml/8 fl oz flat beer
salt and freshly ground black pepper to taste
5 ml/1 teaspoon soft brown sugar
2.5 ml/½ teaspoon wine vinegar
1 bayleaf
1 bouquet garni
25 ml/5 teaspoons plain flour
25 ml/5 teaspoons chopped parsley

Preheat a browning dish on High for 8 minutes. Add the
oil and butter, and microwave on High for 1 minute. Add
the meat, bacon, onion and garlic, and brown on High for
4 minutes. Add the remaining ingredients, except the
flour and parsley, cover, and microwave on Medium-
Low for 40–50 minutes — until the meat is tender.
Remove the bouquet garni and bayleaf. Mix the flour
with a little water into a paste and mix into the casserole,
sprinkle with parsley, and microwave on Medium-Low
for 3 minutes. Stand for about 10 minutes before serving.

COMBINATION OVEN: Cook at 160 °C and medium-low
microwave power level for about 60 minutes (about 1
hour and 40 minutes if your oven alternates convection
and microwave energy).

HUNGARIAN GOULASH

*Serve with Rice (page 21) or noodles (see Pasta, page 43)
and a spinach and avocado salad.*

10 ml/2 teaspoons oil
10 ml/2 teaspoons butter
625 g/1¼ lb topside of beef, cubed
1 onion, chopped
½ red pepper, seeded and sliced
½ green pepper, seeded and sliced
5 tomatoes, peeled and diced
15 ml/1 tablespoon paprika
45 ml/3 tablespoons tomato paste
250 ml/8 fl oz hot beef stock
salt and freshly ground black pepper to taste
200 ml/6½ fl oz plain yoghurt

Preheat a browning dish on High for 8 minutes. Add the
oil and butter, and microwave on High for 1 minute. Add
the meat and onion, and microwave on High for 4
minutes, stirring after 2 minutes. Add the remaining
ingredients, except the yoghurt, mix well, cover, and
microwave on Medium-Low for 40–50 minutes — until
the meat is tender. Stand for about 15 minutes, stir in the
yoghurt and reheat on Medium-Low for 2 minutes.

COMBINATION OVEN: Cook at 160 °C and medium-low
microwave power level for 50–60 minutes (about 1½
hours if your oven alternates between convection and
microwave energy).

STUFFED ROAST LEG OF LAMB

*Serve with Roast Potatoes (page 27) and Vegetable Platter
(page 24). See Hint, pager 24.*

STUFFING
1 onion, chopped
15 ml/1 tablespoon butter
20 ml/4 teaspoons French mustard
60 g/2 oz fresh white breadcrumbs
200 g/6½ oz pork sausagemeat
20 ml/4 teaspoons chopped parsley
5 ml/1 teaspoon grated lemon zest
salt and freshly ground black pepper to taste
10 ml/2 teaspoons chopped fresh
    rosemary
1 egg, beaten

1.5 kg/3 lb leg of lamb, boned
salt and freshly ground black pepper to taste
12.5 ml/2½ teaspoons lemon juice
2 cloves garlic, crushed
20 ml/4 teaspoons oil

Microwave the onion and butter in a bowl on High for
3 minutes. Add the remaining stuffing ingredients and
blend well together. Stuff the pocket of the lamb with the
stuffing and tie securely. Pat the lamb dry, then sprinkle
with seasoning and lemon juice, rub with garlic and brush
with oil. Preheat a browning dish on High for 8 minutes.
Add the lamb and microwave on High for 1 minute per
side, then microwave on Medium-High for 36–42 minutes (12–14 minutes per 500 g/1 lb), turning every 10
minutes. Cover and stand for 10 minutes, then carve.

COMBINATION OVEN: Place the lamb on a greased rack
and cook at 230 °C and medium microwave power level
for 36–42 minutes [12–14 minutes per 500 g/1 lb] (48–
54 minutes [14–16 minutes per 500 g/1 lb] if your oven
alternates convection and microwave energy).

Hungarian Goulash (page 28) and Fruity Lamb Roast (page 30).

SPECIAL GRAVY

A tasty gravy that will enhance any roast meat.

2 carrots, peeled and sliced
1 large onion, chopped
2 sticks celery, chopped
30 ml/2 tablespoons oil
25 ml/5 teaspoons plain flour
750 ml/24 fl oz hot chicken stock
7.5 ml/1½ teaspoons tomato paste
few sprigs of parsley
1 bayleaf
8 peppercorns
salt to taste
12.5 ml/2½ teaspoons sherry
25 ml/5 teaspoons single cream
5 ml/1 teaspoon lemon juice

In a large glass bowl, microwave the carrots, onion, celery and oil on High for 4 minutes. Stir in the flour, then add the stock, tomato paste, parsley, bayleaf and peppercorns. Microwave on High for 5 minutes, then on Medium for 15–20 minutes. Strain the gravy through a sieve. Stir in the salt, sherry, cream and lemon juice. Serve immediately or, if made in advance, pour the gravy into a vacuum flask to keep it hot.

FRUITY LAMB ROAST

Roast lamb is always a treat!

1.5 kg/3 lb leg of lamb, boned
1 onion, chopped
5 ml/1 teaspoon grated fresh ginger
2 cloves garlic, crushed
440 g/14 oz canned crushed pineapple
100 ml/3½ fl oz white wine vinegar
25 ml/5 teaspoons soy sauce
15 ml/1 tablespoon cornflour
15 ml/1 tablespoon water
25 ml/5 teaspoon soft brown sugar

Open out the lamb, flatten, and place in a dish. Mix the onion, ginger, garlic, pineapple with liquid, vinegar and soy sauce together. Pour the mixture over the lamb and leave to marinate for at least 6 hours.

Drain the meat, reserving the marinade, and pat dry. Preheat a browning dish on High for 8 minutes. Add the meat and brown on High for 2 minutes on each side, then microwave on Medium-High for 36–42 minutes (12–14 minutes per 500 g/1 lb, depending on how well cooked you like your lamb), turning every 10 minutes. Transfer to a serving dish and leave to stand before carving.

To make the gravy, blend the cornflour and water in a jug. Mix in the reserved marinade, the cooking juices from the browning dish and the sugar. Microwave on High for 3–4 minutes, stirring often — until thickened. Serve piping hot.

COMBINATION OVEN: Place the lamb on a rack and brush with oil. Cook at 230 °C and medium microwave power level for 30–36 minutes [10–12 minutes per 500 g/1 lb] (45 minutes [15 minutes per 500 g/1 lb] if your oven alternates convection and microwave energy).

LAMB NAVARIN

This simple lamb and vegetable casserole is a complete meal in itself.

10 small pickling onions, peeled
125 g/4 oz rindless bacon rashers, chopped
2 turnips, peeled and diced
2 carrots, peeled and sliced
10 new potatoes, peeled
100 ml/3½ fl oz water
750 g/1½ lb leg of lamb, boned and cubed
1 clove garlic, crushed
30 ml/2 tablespoons plain flour
315 ml/½ pint hot beef stock
25 ml/5 teaspoons tomato paste
2.5 ml/½ teaspoon black pepper
125 g/4 oz frozen peas
salt to taste
chopped parsley to garnish

In a small bowl, microwave the pickling onions and bacon on High for 4–5 minutes, stirring twice. Set aside. In another bowl, microwave the turnips, carrots and new potatoes with the water on High, covered, for about 6–8 minutes. Set aside.

Preheat a browning dish on High for 8 minutes. Pat the lamb dry and add to the dish. Microwave on High for 4 minutes, stirring after 2 minutes. Add the garlic to the cooking juices, then stir in the flour. Gradually stir in the stock, tomato paste and black pepper. Cover and microwave on Medium-Low for 20 minutes. Stir, then add the onion and bacon. Drain the cooked vegetables and add them to the stew with the peas. Cover and microwave on Medium-Low for another 30 minutes. Check that the meat and vegetables are tender — they may need further cooking. Stand for about 10 minutes. Stir in the salt, sprinkle with fresh parsley and serve.

COMBINATION OVEN: Cook at 160 °C and medium-low microwave power level for 50 minutes (90 minutes if your oven alternates convection and microwave energy).

Rice (page 21) and Lamb Navarin (page 30).

LAMB CURRY WITH POTATOES

*Make this simple curry as hot as you wish by adding more
curry powder. Serve with Rice (page 21).*

> 30 ml/2 tablespoons oil
> 750 g/1½ lb stewing lamb, cubed
> 1 onion, chopped
> 2 cloves garlic, crushed
> 1 bayleaf
> 10–20 ml/2–4 teaspoons curry powder
> 1 tomato, peeled and chopped
> 5 ml/1 teaspoon caster sugar
> 2 potatoes, peeled, cubed and par-cooked
> 45 ml/3 tablespoons water (if necessary)
> fresh coriander leaves to garnish

Preheat a browning dish on High for 8 minutes. Add the
oil and microwave on High for 1 minute. Pat the meat dry
and add to the dish with the onion and garlic. Microwave
on High for 4 minutes, stirring after 2 minutes. Add the
bayleaf and curry powder. Microwave on High for 2
minutes; cover and microwave on Medium-Low for 35
minutes. Add the tomato, sugar and potatoes; microwave
on Medium-Low for 20–25 minutes, adding water if
needed — until the potatoes are cooked. Stand for about
8 minutes. Serve, garnished with coriander leaves.

COMBINATION OVEN: Cook at 160 °C and medium–low
microwave power level for about 60 minutes (about 90
minutes if your oven alternates convection and microwave energy).

VARIATION: Turn this into an exotically spicy dish by
adding 5 ml/1 teaspoon each turmeric, ground coriander
and ground ginger, 45 ml/3 tablespoons sultanas, 2 apples
(peeled, cored and chopped) and 30 ml/2 tablespoons
chutney when you add the curry powder.

LAMB BOURGUIGNONNE

750 g/1½ lb leg of lamb, boned and cubed
200 g/6½ oz rindless streaky bacon, diced
25 ml/5 teaspoons plain flour
200 ml/6½ fl oz hot beef stock
100 ml/3½ fl oz red wine
1 bayleaf
salt and freshly ground black pepper to taste
5 ml/1 teaspoon dried rosemary
200 g/6½ oz pickling onions, peeled
200 g/6½ oz button mushrooms

Preheat a browning dish on High for 8 minutes. Add the lamb and bacon, and microwave on High for 4 minutes, stirring after 1 minute. Stir in the flour, then gradually stir in the stock and wine. Add the bayleaf, seasoning and rosemary. Cover and microwave on Medium-Low for 30 minutes. Stir in the onions and mushrooms, and microwave on High for 10–15 minutes — until the meat is tender. Stand for about 10 minutes, remove the bayleaf and serve piping hot.

COMBINATION OVEN: Cook at 160 °C and medium-low power level for 40–45 minutes (about 90 minutes if your oven alternates convection and microwave energy).

VEAL WITH VEGETABLE SAUCE

Baked potatoes make a good accompaniment.

4 veal escalopes (about 440 g/14 oz),
      beaten flat
pinch of dried herbs
salt and freshly ground black pepper to taste
3 spring onions, chopped
100 ml/3½ fl oz tomato purée (passata)
2.5 ml/½ teaspoon dried basil
2.5 ml/½ teaspoon dried oregano
12.5 ml/2½ teaspoons chopped parsley
1 clove garlic, crushed
3 courgettes, sliced
2 medium tomatoes, peeled and chopped
5 ml/1 teaspoon caster sugar

Preheat a browning dish on High for 8 minutes. Dust the veal with herbs and pepper, and add to the dish. Microwave on High for 1 minute, turn over, and microwave on High for about 6 minutes. Transfer the veal to a serving dish and cover to keep warm. Add the remaining ingredients to the dish, and microwave on High for 6–8 minutes — until the vegetables are tender. Pour the sauce over the veal and serve immediately.

Veal with Vegetable Sauce (this page) and Apricot Pork Casserole (page 33).

VEAL WITH PEPPERCORN SAUCE

625 g/1¼ lb veal schnitzels, cut into
    5-cm/2-inch strips
15 ml/1 tablespoon oil
15 g/½ oz butter
salt and freshly ground black pepper to taste

PEPPERCORN SAUCE
30 g/1 oz butter
45 ml/3 tablespoons plain flour
500 ml/16 fl oz milk
30 ml/2 tablespoons green peppercorns
60 ml/4 tablespoons dry white wine
5 ml/1 teaspoon salt
2.5 ml/½ teaspoon freshly grated nutmeg

Pat the meat dry. Preheat a browning dish on High for 8 minutes. Add the oil and butter, then the veal. Microwave on High for 5–6 minutes, stirring twice. Transfer the veal to a serving dish and season. To make the sauce, add the butter to the browning dish and microwave on High for 30 seconds to melt. Stir in the flour, then gradually add the milk. Microwave on High for 5–6 minutes, stirring twice — until thickened. Stir in the peppercorns, wine, salt and nutmeg. Pour the sauce over the veal, microwave on High for 2 minutes, then serve.

VEAL AND MUSHROOM CASSEROLE

500–750 g/1–1½ lb veal, cubed
22 g/¾ oz butter
1 onion, finely chopped
1 clove garlic, crushed
25 ml/5 teaspoons plain flour
250 ml/8 fl oz hot chicken stock
100 ml/3½ fl oz sherry
5 ml/1 teaspoon Worcestershire sauce
2.5 ml/½ teaspoon paprika
white pepper to taste
200 g/6½ oz button mushrooms, sliced
155 ml/¼ pint soured cream
salt to taste
15 ml/1 tablespoon chopped parsley

Pat the meat dry. Preheat a browning dish on High for 8 minutes. Add the butter, then the meat. Microwave on High for 4 minutes, stirring after 2 minutes. Remove the meat, and add the onion and garlic. Microwave on High for 3 minutes. Stir in the flour, then gradually stir in the stock, sherry and Worcestershire sauce. Add the paprika and pepper, mix in the meat, then microwave, covered, on Medium-Low for 20 minutes. Add the mushrooms and microwave on Medium-Low for another 20–45 minutes — until the meat is tender. Stand for 10 minutes, stir in the cream and salt, sprinkle with parsley and serve.

COMBINATION OVEN: Cook at 160 °C and medium-low microwave power level for 40–45 minutes (60 minutes if your oven alternates convection and microwave energy).

APRICOT PORK CASSEROLE

22 g/¾ oz butter
1 onion, sliced
25 ml/5 teaspoons plain flour
1 red pepper, seeded and sliced
100 g/3½ oz dried apricots
440 g/14 oz pork fillet, cubed
2 tomatoes, peeled and chopped
5 ml/1 teaspoon Worcestershire sauce
5 ml/1 teaspoon soft brown sugar
125 ml/4 fl oz apricot juice
salt and freshly ground black pepper to taste
5 ml/1 teaspoon dried thyme

Microwave the butter and onion in a bowl on High for 3 minutes. Stir in the flour. Add the red pepper, apricots, pork fillet, tomatoes, Worcestershire sauce and sugar. Pour the apricot juice over, season and top with thyme. Cover and microwave on High for 6 minutes. Stir, then microwave on Medium-Low for 30 minutes. Check seasoning, stand for 10 minutes and serve.

SWEET AND SOUR PORK SAUSAGES

500 g/1 lb pork sausages, pierced
15 g/½ oz butter
1 onion, chopped
410 g/13 oz canned pineapple pieces,
    with 100 ml/3½ fl oz of the juice
45 ml/3 tablespoons red wine vinegar
45 ml/3 tablespoons tomato paste
75 g/2½ oz soft brown sugar
5 ml/1 teaspoon mustard powder
25 ml/5 teaspoons cornflour
pinch of salt

Pat the sausages dry. Microwave the butter and onion on High for 2 minutes. Add the remaining ingredients (except the sausages) and microwave on High for 3–4 minutes — until the sauce thickens. Cover to keep warm.
    Preheat a browning dish on High for 8 minutes. Add the sausages and microwave on High for 1 minute. Turn over and microwave on High for 5 minutes. Place the sausages in a serving dish, pour the sauce over and serve.

CHAPTER THREE

Chicken

CHICKEN is always a popular choice. Cooking chicken in the microwave will not only save you time but it will also keep the flesh tender and juicy. This interesting selection of tasty recipes shows how versatile microwave cooking can be.

NOTES

◆ Defrost chicken completely before cooking.
◆ Always cook chicken thoroughly. To check if a whole chicken is cooked, insert a skewer into the flesh. If the juices are pink, the chicken is not completely cooked.
◆ If you are going to stuff chicken, put the stuffing in just before cooking to prevent contamination.
◆ Truss a whole chicken to ensure even cooking.
◆ Season chicken with salt before cooking.
◆ Let chicken stand for 10–15 minutes before carving.
◆ Cook a whole chicken on High for 10–12 minutes per 500 g/1 lb, and pieces on High for 8–10 minutes per 500 g/1 lb.

CHICKEN AND VEGETABLE SOUP

1 kg/2 lb whole chicken or chicken pieces
250 ml/8 fl oz water
1 onion, chopped
2 sticks celery, chopped
1 carrot and 1 turnip, peeled and diced
30 ml/2 tablespoons water
1.5 litres/2¾ pints hot chicken stock
100 g/3½ oz noodles
30 ml/2 tablespoons chopped parsley

Place the chicken and 250 ml/8 fl oz water in a large casserole and microwave on High for 5 minutes; cover and microwave on High for 10 minutes. Place the vegetables and 30 ml/2 tablespoons water in a dish, cover and microwave on High for 10 minutes. Add the cooked vegetables to the chicken and stir in the stock and noodles. Microwave, covered, on High for 10 minutes, then on Medium for 10 minutes. Remove the chicken and skim the excess fat from the soup. Remove the skin and bones from the chicken and discard. Chop the flesh into pieces and add as much as required to the soup. Reheat on High for a few minutes, sprinkle with parsley and serve.

CREAMED CHICKEN AND POTATO BAKE

Keep cooked chicken in the freezer for a quick meal.

30 g/1 oz butter
2 onions, chopped
315 g/10 oz button mushrooms, sliced
5 ml/1 teaspoon dried mixed herbs
salt and freshly ground black pepper to taste
45 ml/3 tablespoons plain flour
500 ml/16 fl oz hot chicken stock
25 ml/5 teaspoons dry sherry
315 g/10 oz cooked chicken, diced
125 ml/4 fl oz soured cream
5 ml/1 teaspoon Worcestershire sauce

TOPPING
500 g/1 lb potatoes, peeled and thinly sliced
100 ml/3½ fl oz water
60 g/2 oz Cheddar or Gruyère cheese, grated
paprika to taste

Microwave the butter and onions in a bowl on High for 5 minutes. Add the mushrooms, dried herbs and seasoning and microwave on High for 3 minutes. Stir in the flour and gradually add the stock and sherry. Microwave on High for 5 minutes, stirring twice. Add the chicken, soured cream and Worcestershire sauce, and place the mixture in a casserole.

In a bowl, microwave the potatoes and water on High for 5 minutes. Stand for 10 minutes, drain, pat dry and arrange over the chicken. Sprinkle with cheese and paprika; microwave on Medium-High for 15–20 minutes. Stand for 5 minutes, then serve.

COMBINATION OVEN: Cook at 220 °C and medium microwave power level for about 20 minutes (about 30 minutes if your oven alternates convection and microwave energy).

Baked Chicken and Broccoli (page 36) and Creamed Chicken and Potato Bake (page 34).

BAKED CHICKEN AND BROCCOLI

4 chicken breasts
1 bayleaf
250 ml/8 fl oz hot chicken stock
500 g/1 lb broccoli, broken into florets
410 g/13 oz canned cream of chicken soup
60 ml/4 tablespoons mayonnaise
60 ml/4 tablespoons plain yoghurt
100 g/3½ oz Cheddar cheese, grated
5 ml/1 teaspoon lemon juice
5–10 ml/1–2 teaspoons curry powder

TOPPING
25 ml/5 teaspoons dried breadcrumbs, seasoned
60 g/2 oz Cheddar cheese, grated
30 ml/2 tablespoons chopped parsley
paprika to taste

Microwave the chicken with the bayleaf and stock on High for 8–10 minutes — until just cooked. Remove the chicken and slice into slivers. Strain and reserve the stock. Mix the broccoli with the chicken in a casserole. Mix the soup, reserved stock, mayonnaise, yoghurt, cheese, lemon juice and curry powder together, and pour over the chicken and broccoli. Mix the breadcrumbs, cheese and parsley together, and sprinkle over the chicken. Dust with paprika, then microwave on Medium-High for 8–10 minutes. Stand for 5 minutes before serving.

COMBINATION OVEN: Cook at 200 °C and medium microwave power level for about 14 minutes (about 20 minutes if your oven alternates convection and microwave energy).

STIR-FRIED CHICKEN

Serve with Rice (page 21) or Pasta (page 43).

MARINADE
1 clove garlic, crushed
5 ml/1 teaspoon grated fresh ginger
20 ml/4 teaspoons soy sauce
20 ml/4 teaspoons medium sherry
20 ml/4 teaspoons soft brown sugar
½ chicken stock cube, crumbled
pinch of freshly ground black pepper

3 chicken breasts, filleted and cut into strips
12.5 ml/2½ teaspoons oil
2 carrots, peeled and cut in julienne strips
155 g/5 oz button mushrooms, sliced
60 g/2 oz bean sprouts
100 g/3½ oz fresh broccoli, cut into florets

Mix the marinade ingredients together well, then mix in the chicken. Set aside for 1 hour.

Preheat a browning dish on High for 6 minutes. Add the oil, carrots, mushrooms, sprouts and broccoli, and microwave on High for 2–3 minutes, stirring frequently. Remove the vegetables from the dish and add the strips of marinated chicken. Microwave on High for 4–5 minutes, stirring frequently — until the chicken is tender. Add the cooked vegetables to the dish, mix in, then microwave on High for 1–2 minutes to heat through. Serve as suggested.

VARIATION: About 440 g/14 oz rump steak, cut into strips, can be used instead of the chicken.

FRENCH CHICKEN CASSEROLE

A creamy casserole with the flavour of apples which epitomizes the gastronomic tradition of Normandy. Serve it with Rice (page 21).

1 kg/2 lb chicken pieces
45 ml/3 tablespoons seasoned flour
20 ml/4 teaspoons oil
22 g/¾ oz butter
45 ml/3 tablespoons dry white wine
2 Granny Smith apples, peeled, cored and chopped
3 sticks celery, thinly sliced
1 onion, finely chopped
sprig of parsley
pinch of salt
2.5 ml/½ teaspoon paprika
15 ml/1 tablespoon cornflour
315 ml/½ pint hot chicken stock
75 ml/2½ fl oz soured cream
10 ml/2 teaspoons chopped fresh tarragon

Dust the chicken pieces with the flour. Preheat a browning dish on High for about 8 minutes. Add the oil and butter and microwave on High for 1 minute, then add the chicken and microwave on High for 5 minutes, turning the chicken over after 2½ minutes. Remove the chicken and drain the oil from the browning dish. Add the wine to the dish and microwave on High for 1 minute. Stir in the apples, celery, onion, parsley, salt and paprika. Cover and microwave on High for 6 minutes. Mix the cornflour into a paste with a little water, then stir in the stock and add to the mixture in the browning dish. Microwave on High for 2–3 minutes — until the sauce has thickened. Add the chicken to the dish, coating it in the sauce. Cover and microwave on Medium-High for 30 minutes. Stir in the soured cream and tarragon, then serve the casserole as suggested with rice.

Stir-Fried Chicken (page 36) and Spicy Chicken Curry (page 38).

BAKED CHICKEN MONTE CARLO

1.5 kg/3 lb whole chicken
chicken seasoning to taste
345 g/11 oz fresh broccoli, broken into florets
45 ml/3 tablespoons water
salt and pepper to taste
pinch of freshly grated nutmeg
315 g/10 oz mushrooms or asparagus, sliced
30 g/1 oz butter
salt and freshly ground black pepper to taste

PARISIENNE SAUCE
75 g/2½ oz butter
60 g/2 oz plain flour, sifted
750 ml/24 fl oz hot chicken stock
2.5 ml/½ teaspoon salt

45 ml/3 tablespoons grated Parmesan cheese

Sprinkle the chicken with chicken seasoning, place in a cooking bag and tie loosely. Place the bag on a saucer in a casserole and microwave on High for 5 minutes, then on Medium-High for 15–20 minutes. Stand for 10 minutes, then drain and cool. Skin the chicken and slice the flesh into bite-sized pieces.

Microwave the broccoli and water, covered, on High for 6 minutes, stand for 3 minutes, then drain and sprinkle with seasoning and nutmeg.

Place the mushrooms or asparagus and butter in a bowl and microwave on High for 4 minutes. Season.

To make the sauce, microwave the butter in a bowl on High for 1 minute. Stir in the flour and stock, season, then microwave on High for 4–6 minutes, stirring twice.

Place the broccoli in a deep, round casserole, pour half the sauce over and sprinkle with a little cheese. Layer with the mushrooms, arrange the chicken on top, and pour the rest of the sauce over. Sprinkle with the remaining cheese. Microwave on Medium–High for 10 minutes.

Chicken Pilaff (this page) and Coq au Vin (page 39).

SPICY CHICKEN CURRY

This dish improves with keeping — so it may be made in advance and then reheated before serving.

> 30 g/1 oz butter
> 2 onions, chopped
> 1 green or red pepper, seeded and chopped
> 5 ml/1 teaspoon curry powder
> 45 g/1½ oz chicken noodle soup powder
> 60 g/2 oz frozen peas
> 60 ml/4 tablespoons seedless raisins
> 2.5 ml/½ teaspoon ground ginger
> 12.5 ml/2½ teaspoons tomato paste
> /50 ml/24 fl oz hot chicken stock
> 2 whole chickens, cooked, boned and divided
>   into pieces (see Notes, page 34)

In a glass bowl, microwave the butter, onions and pepper on High for 5 minutes. Stir in the curry powder and microwave on High for 1 minute. Add the soup powder, peas, raisins, ginger, tomato paste and stock. Microwave, covered, on Medium for 10 minutes. Add the chicken, cover, and microwave on Medium for 10 minutes.

CHICKEN PILAFF

> 12.5 ml/2½ teaspoons oil
> 30 g/1 oz butter
> 1 onion, chopped
> 4 chicken breasts, skinned, boned and sliced
> 200 g/6½ oz rice
> 500 ml/16 fl oz boiling water
> 1 chicken stock cube, crumbled
> good pinch of ground ginger
> ½ green pepper, seeded and chopped
> 1 tomato, peeled and chopped
> 12.5 ml/2½ teaspoons chopped parsley

Preheat a browning dish on High for 8 minutes. Add the oil and butter, and microwave on High for 30 seconds. Mix in the onion and chicken, and microwave on High for 3 minutes. Add the rice and microwave on High for 35 minutes. Stir in the water, stock cube and ginger; microwave, uncovered, on High for 10–15 minutes, stirring lightly twice. Add the green pepper and tomato, and microwave on High for 5–7 minutes. Leave to stand, covered, for 10–15 minutes, then garnish with fresh parsley and serve hot.

CHICKEN AND VEGETABLE CASSEROLE

This is an ideal dish for a low-fat diet. Serve with Mashed Potato (page 14) or Rice (page 21).

2 sticks celery, sliced
1 large onion, chopped
500 g/1 lb carrots, peeled and thinly sliced
5 ml/1 teaspoon dried mixed herbs
100 ml/3½ fl oz hot chicken stock
100 ml/3½ fl oz dry white wine
salt and freshly ground black pepper to taste
250 g/8 oz broccoli, broken into florets
1 kg/2 lb chicken pieces, skinned
200 g/6½ oz button mushrooms, quartered
12.5 ml/2½ teaspoons plain flour or
    60 g/2 oz onion soup powder

Place the celery, onion, carrots, herbs, stock, wine, seasoning and broccoli in a deep casserole. Cover and microwave on High for 6 minutes. Add the chicken and mushrooms, and mix well. Cover and microwave on Medium-Low for 20–25 minutes. To thicken, mix the flour to a paste with a little water and stir in, or stir in the soup powder. Cover and microwave on Medium-Low for another 10 minutes. Stand for 10 minutes before serving as suggested above.

COMBINATION OVEN: Cook at 200 °C and medium microwave power level for about 35 minutes (about 50 minutes if your oven alternates convection and microwave energy).

COQ AU VIN

A well-known French dish that is superb when cooked in a microwave.

60 ml/4 tablespoons plain flour
2.5 ml/½ teaspoon lemon pepper
2.5 ml/½ teaspoon paprika
5 ml/1 teaspoon chicken seasoning
1 kg/2 lb chicken pieces
45 ml/3 tablespoons oil
30 g/1 oz butter
15 pickling onions, peeled
2 cloves garlic, crushed
125 g/4 oz rindless bacon rashers, chopped
200 g/6½ oz button mushrooms, quartered
440 g/14 oz canned chopped tomatoes
salt and freshly ground black pepper to taste
2 bayleaves
200 ml/6½ fl oz dry red wine
100 ml/3½ fl oz hot chicken stock
30 ml/2 tablespoons chopped parsley

Mix the flour, lemon pepper, paprika and chicken seasoning together. Coat the chicken pieces in the flour mixture. Keep the excess flour to thicken the sauce.

Preheat a browning dish on High for 7 minutes. Add the oil and butter, and microwave on High for 1 minute. Add the chicken pieces; microwave on High for 5 minutes, turning them over halfway. Remove the chicken and add the onions, garlic and bacon to the dish. Microwave on High for 3–4 minutes, stirring twice. Mix in the mushrooms, tomatoes and any remaining flour; stir well. Mix in the seasoning, bayleaves, wine and stock. Microwave on High for 5–7 minutes, stirring twice — until the sauce thickens. Add the chicken, coating it with the sauce. Cover and microwave on Medium-High for 25–30 minutes — until the chicken is tender. Stand for 5 minutes, then garnish with parsley and serve.

SAVOURY RICE

200 g/6½ oz rice
625 ml/1 pint boiling water
1 chicken stock cube
25 ml/5 teaspoons tomato sauce
2.5 ml/1 teaspoon salt

Place the rice and water in a large bowl, cover, and leave to soak for 20 minutes. Add the remaining ingredients and microwave on High for 5 minutes, then on Medium for 10 minutes. Stand for 15 minutes, then serve.

NOTE: The amount of water used depends on the brand of rice; some require more than others.

CURRIED CHICKEN WITH FRUIT

1.5 kg/3 lb chicken pieces
chicken seasoning to taste
200 ml/6½ fl oz fresh orange juice
25 ml/5 teaspoons lemon juice
60 ml/4 tablespoons clear honey
15–20 ml/3–4 teaspoons curry powder
1 Granny Smith apple, peeled, cored and
    chopped

Preheat a browning dish on High for 8 minutes. Season the chicken and add to the browning dish. Microwave on High for 2½ minutes per side. Turn the chicken skin-side down. Mix together the orange juice, lemon juice, honey, curry powder and apple. Pour the mixture over the chicken, cover, and microwave on Medium for 30–35 minutes — until the chicken is cooked through. Stand for about 10 minutes, then serve.

HAWAIIAN CHICKEN

1.5 kg/3 lb whole chicken
100 ml/3½ fl oz soy sauce
75 ml/2½ fl oz pineapple juice

Place the chicken on a roasting rack in a dish. Mix the soy and pineapple juice together and brush over the chicken. Microwave on High for 5 minutes, then on Medium-High for 30 minutes. Baste a few times during cooking.

COMBINATION OVEN: Cook on 220 °C and medium microwave power level for about 30 minutes [10 minutes per 500 g/1 lb chicken] (about 45 minutes [15 minutes per 500 g/1 lb chicken] if your oven alternates convection and microwave energy).

CURRIED CHICKEN WITH PEACHES

Serve hot with Rice (page 21) and a crisp salad.

8 chicken breasts, boned
60 ml/4 tablespoons fruit chutney
45 ml/3 tablespoons clear honey
10 ml/2 teaspoons curry powder
1 onion, finely chopped
100 ml/3½ fl oz mayonnaise
410 g/13 oz canned sliced peaches in juice

Place the chicken in a shallow dish. Mix together the chutney, honey, curry powder, onion and mayonnaise. Drain the peaches and add the juice to the chutney mixture. Pour over the chicken. Cover and microwave on Medium-High for about 16 minutes. Uncover and add the peach slices. Microwave on High for 5–6 minutes.

BASIC BREAD STUFFING

30 g/1 oz butter
1 onion, chopped
125 g/4 oz fresh breadcrumbs
12.5 ml/2½ teaspoons chopped parsley
45 ml/3 tablespoons milk
2.5 ml/½ teaspoon dried thyme
salt to taste
2.5 ml/½ teaspoon pepper
1 egg

In a bowl, microwave the butter and onion on High for 4–5 minutes. Add the breadcrumbs, parsley, milk, thyme, salt, pepper and egg, and combine thoroughly. Stuff the chicken just before cooking.

ROAST CHICKEN WITH WALDORF STUFFING AND GRAVY

WALDORF STUFFING
22 g/¾ oz butter
1 onion, chopped
60 ml/4 tablespoons chopped walnuts
2 sticks celery, chopped
1 large apple, cored and chopped
45 ml/3 tablespoons seedless raisins
25 ml/5 teaspoons chopped parsley
1 egg, lightly beaten
salt and freshly ground black pepper to taste
pinch of cinnamon
60 g/2 oz fresh breadcrumbs

1.5 kg/3 lb whole chicken
10 ml/2 teaspoons oil
10 ml/2 teaspoons melted butter
paprika to taste
ground coriander to taste

GRAVY
25 ml/5 teaspoons plain flour
250 ml/8 fl oz hot chicken stock
dash of Worcestershire sauce
2.5 ml/½ teaspoon dried mixed herbs
freshly ground black pepper to taste

First make the stuffing. In a bowl, microwave the butter, onion, walnuts and celery on High for 4–5 minutes. Add the apple, raisins, parsley, egg, seasoning, cinnamon and breadcrumbs. Mix well.

Rinse the chicken inside and out, and pat dry with a paper towel. Stuff the body cavity and neck cavity with the stuffing and truss the chicken. Brush with the oil and melted butter, and sprinkle with paprika and coriander.

Preheat a browning dish on High for 8 minutes. Place the chicken, breast-side down, in the dish and microwave on High for 3 minutes. Turn and microwave on High for 2 minutes, then microwave on Medium-High for 30 minutes — until cooked. Remove the chicken from the rack. Stand for 10 minutes before carving.

To make the gravy, stir the flour into the cooking juices in the browning dish and microwave on High for 1–2 minutes. Stir in the stock, Worcestershire sauce, herbs and pepper, and microwave on High for 3–4 minutes. Pour into a serving jug and serve hot.

COMBINATION OVEN: Place on a roasting rack on the turntable or in a roasting pan. Pour a little water on to the turntable or into the roasting pan. Cook on 230 °C and medium microwave power level for 30 minutes [10 minutes per 500 g/1 lb chicken] (about 45 minutes [15 minutes per 500 g/1 lb] if your oven alternates convection and microwave energy).

Roast Chicken with Waldorf Stuffing and Gravy (page 40).

ROAST CHICKEN WITH ORANGE SAUCE

Citrus Rice (page 14) and green beans make the perfect accompaniments to this delicious roast chicken.

> 1 large whole chicken
> 1 orange (with skin), sliced into rounds
> 5 ml / 1 teaspoon chicken seasoning
>
> ORANGE SAUCE
> 15 g / ½ oz butter
> 250 ml / 8 fl oz fresh orange juice
> 90 g / 3 oz caster sugar
> 5 ml / 1 teaspoon grated lemon zest
> 12.5 ml / 2½ teaspoons cornflour
> 75 ml / 2½ fl oz milk
> 12.5 ml / 2½ teaspoons Grand Marnier or
>   Cointreau (optional)

Pat the chicken dry with a paper towel. Carefully lift the skin up off the breasts with your fingers and slide the orange slices under the skin. Rub the chicken seasoning over the chicken. Preheat a browning dish on High for 8 minutes. Place the chicken in the dish, breast-side down, and microwave on High for 2 minutes. Turn and microwave on High for 3 minutes, then microwave on Medium-High for 10 minutes per 500 g / 1 lb chicken, basting often.

To make the sauce, microwave the butter, orange juice, sugar and lemon zest in a bowl on High for 3 minutes, stirring to dissolve the sugar. Mix the cornflour and milk to a paste and add to the orange mixture. Microwave on High for 2 minutes, stirring once — until the mixture thickens. Add the liqueur, if using, and pour into a serving jug. Serve hot.

COMBINATION OVEN: Brush the chicken with melted butter and cook at 220 °C and medium microwave power level for 10 minutes per 500 g / 1 lb (15 minutes per 500 g / 1 lb if your oven alternates convection and microwave energy), turning halfway and basting often.

VARIATIONS: Instead of slices of orange, use pats of creamed herb butter or garlic butter. Cream the butter with chopped fresh herbs or garlic, then refrigerate to firm.

Spaghetti Vongole (page 43).

CHAPTER FOUR

Pasta & vegetarian

PASTA AND VEGETARIAN dishes are wonderful to cook quickly in the microwave and can be so imaginatively prepared. Pasta is a major source of energy; vegetables not only provide a wealth of vitamins and minerals but also make a filling meal.

PASTA

Cook the pasta, then make the sauce while the pasta is standing, or make the sauce first and reheat on High for a few minutes before serving, or cook the pasta on the hob while you make the sauce in the microwave oven.

> 250 g/8 oz pasta
> 1 litre/1¾ pints boiling water
> 5 ml/1 teaspoon salt
> 5 ml/1 teaspoon oil

Place all the ingredients in a large glass or plastic bowl. Microwave on High for 5–6 minutes for small pasta shapes (such as vermicelli), 6–8 minutes for medium pasta shapes (such as spaghetti, tagliatelle, fettucini and elbow macaroni), and 10–12 minutes for large pasta shapes (such as macaroni, fusilli, shell and penne). Stand, covered, for about 5 minutes, then drain and use.

If pasta is frozen, defrost, then reheat on High for 2–3 minutes.

CREAMY TROUT SAUCE WITH PASTA

Trout fillets are now available at most supermarkets. This simple, tasty sauce can be served with pasta of your choice.

> 4 smoked trout fillets
> 1 onion, chopped
> 30 g/1 oz butter
> 25 ml/5 teaspoons plain flour
> 315 ml/½ pint hot Fish Stock (page 6)
> pinch of dried dill
> 5 ml/1 teaspoon lemon juice
> salt and freshly ground black pepper to taste
> 45 ml/3 tablespoons Greek yoghurt
>   (optional)
> 250 g/8 oz pasta of your choice, cooked
>   (see Pasta, above)

Flake the trout fillets roughly. Microwave the onion and butter on High for 3 minutes. Stir in the flour, then gradually stir in the stock, dill and lemon juice. Microwave on High for 4 minutes, stirring twice for a smooth sauce. Gently mix in the trout and season to taste. Stir in the yoghurt, if using, then microwave on Medium-High for 3–5 minutes. Keep warm while you cook the pasta. Spoon sauce over pasta to serve.

SPAGHETTI VONGOLE

This is one of the most popular of Italian dishes.

> 1 onion, finely chopped
> 2 cloves garlic, crushed
> 45 ml/3 tablespoons olive oil
> 440 g/14 oz canned chopped tomatoes
> 12.5 ml/2½ teaspoons tomato paste
> 100 ml/3½ fl oz dry white wine
> 280 g/9 oz canned clams, drained
> 30 ml/2 tablespoons chopped parsley
> 10 ml/2 teaspoons chopped fresh basil
> salt and freshly ground black pepper to taste
> 315 g/10 oz spaghetti, cooked (see
>   Pasta, this page)

Microwave the onion, garlic and oil in a bowl on High for 3 minutes. Stir in the tomatoes with liquid, tomato purée and wine, and microwave on High for 15 minutes — until thick and pulpy. Mix in the clams, cover and microwave on High for 3 minutes. Stir in the parsley and basil, and season. Keep warm while you cook the spaghetti.

Mix the sauce into the spaghetti and serve piping hot.

VARIATION: If fresh clams are available, add 315 g/10 oz to the tomato and wine sauce and microwave on High for about 5 minutes or until all the clams have opened. Discard any that don't open.

HAM AND MUSHROOM PASTA PIE

250 g/8 oz macaroni pieces, cooked
(see Pasta, page 43)
315 g/10 oz button mushrooms, sliced
45 g/1½ oz butter
1 clove garlic, crushed
30 g/1 oz plain flour
2.5 ml/½ teaspoon mustard powder
500 ml/16 fl oz milk
100 g/3½ oz Cheddar cheese, grated
salt and freshly ground black pepper to taste
125 g/4 oz ham, diced
2 eggs, beaten
25 ml/5 teaspoons dried breadcrumbs,
seasoned
paprika to taste
chopped parsley to garnish

Cook the macaroni pieces. Make the sauce while the macaroni is standing.

In a bowl, microwave the mushrooms, butter and garlic on High for 3 minutes. Stir in the flour and mustard, then gradually stir in the milk. Microwave on High for about 5 minutes — until the sauce thickens. Stir in 75 g/2½ oz of the cheese and the seasoning. Drain the macaroni and mix into the sauce with the ham and eggs. Pour the mixture into a deep casserole. Top with the remaining cheese and sprinkle with the breadcrumbs and paprika. Microwave on Medium-High for 12–14 minutes. Stand for 3–4 minutes, garnish with parsley and serve.

COMBINATION OVEN: Cook on 200 °C and medium-low microwave power level for 15 minutes (20–25 minutes if your oven alternates convection and microwave energy).

LUSCIOUS LASAGNE

250 g/8 oz sheets of spinach lasagne,
cooked (see Pasta, page 43)
10 ml/2 teaspoons oil
1 clove garlic, crushed
1 large onion, chopped
500 g/1 lb minced beef
125 ml/4 fl oz hot beef stock
75 ml/2½ fl oz red wine
100 ml/3½ fl oz tomato purée (passata)
5 ml/1 teaspoon dried mixed herbs
5 ml/1 teaspoon dried marjoram
5 ml/1 teaspoon dried oregano
5 ml/1 teaspoon caster sugar
15 ml/1 tablespoon cornflour
salt and freshly ground black pepper to taste
250 ml/8 fl oz Cheese Sauce (this page)

Cook the pasta and set aside. To make the meat sauce, place the oil, garlic and onion in a bowl and microwave on High for 4–5 minutes. Add the beef, stock, wine, tomato purée, herbs, sugar, cornflour and seasoning. Stir well, then microwave on Medium for 20 minutes. Stir again and set aside. Make the Cheese Sauce.

Layer half the pasta in a flat-bottomed dish. Top with half the meat sauce, then half the Cheese Sauce. Repeat. Microwave on Medium-High for 10–12 minutes.

If making in advance, cool, then freeze. Defrost for 10–15 minutes — until the centre is no longer icy. Heat through on Medium-High for 10–15 minutes — until the centre is hot. Stand for 5 minutes before serving.

CHEESE SAUCE

45 g/1½ oz butter
45 g/1½ oz plain flour
500 ml/16 fl oz milk
90 g/3 oz Cheddar cheese, grated
pinch of freshly grated nutmeg
salt and freshly ground black pepper to taste
5 ml/1 teaspoon prepared mustard

Microwave the butter for 50 seconds to melt. Stir in the flour, then gradually add the milk. Microwave on High for 5–6 minutes, stirring twice. Stir in the cheese, nutmeg, seasoning and mustard. MAKES ABOUT 500 ML/16 FL OZ.

MACARONI CHEESE DELUXE

250 g/8 oz elbow macaroni, cooked
(see Pasta, page 43)
500 ml/16 fl oz Cheese Sauce (this page)
410 g/13 oz canned chopped tomatoes
with onions
salt and freshly ground black pepper to taste
15 ml/1 tablespoon chopped fresh herbs of your
choice or 5 ml/1 teaspoon dried mixed herbs
45 ml/3 tablespoons grated Cheddar cheese
12.5 ml/2½ teaspoons dried breadcrumbs,
seasoned
paprika to taste

Cook the macaroni, rinse in cold water and set aside. Make the Cheese Sauce. Mix the chopped tomatoes with the seasoning and herbs.

Spoon half of the macaroni into a flat-bottomed dish, top with half the tomato mixture and pour half the Cheese Sauce over. Repeat the layers, then top with the cheese and sprinkle with the breadcrumbs and paprika. Microwave on Medium-High power for 12–14 minutes. Stand for about 4 minutes before serving.

Noodles, Onion and Spinach with Cheese Sauce (page 46) and Ham and Mushroom Pasta Pie (page 44).

EASY TOMATO AND MUSSEL SAUCE FOR PASTA

A simple but tasty treat to serve with pasta! The sauce is made with olive oil in the Mediterranean way.

> 750 g/1½ lb cooked mussels
> 25 ml/5 teaspoons olive oil
> 1 onion, chopped
> 2 cloves garlic, crushed
> 500 g/1 lb tomatoes, peeled and chopped
> 2.5 ml/½ teaspoon sugar
> salt and freshly ground black pepper to taste
> 200 g/6½ oz pasta (such as tagliatelle), cooked (see Pasta, page 43)
> 30 ml/2 tablespoons chopped parsley

Remove the mussels from their shells, reserving a few to garnish. Microwave the oil and onion in a bowl on High for 3–4 minutes. Add the garlic and tomatoes, and microwave on High for 10–12 minutes — until the tomatoes are pulpy. Stir in the sugar, seasoning and the mussels. Microwave on High for 2 minutes. Keep warm while you cook the pasta.

Pile the sauce on top of the pasta. Garnish with the parsley and the reserved mussels before serving.

CREAMY CHICKEN WITH NOODLES

> 250 g/8 oz fusilli, cooked (see Pasta, page 43)
> 1 whole chicken, cooked, boned, skinned and cubed
> 1 chicken stock cube, crumbled
> 200 g/6½ oz canned creamed sliced mushrooms
> 45 ml/3 tablespoons sherry
> 25 ml/5 teaspoons plain flour, sifted
> salt and freshly ground black pepper to taste
> 100 ml/3½ fl oz single cream
> 30 ml/2 tablespoons grated Parmesan cheese
> 30 ml/2 tablespoons chopped parsley
> pinch of paprika

Cook the pasta. Make the sauce while the pasta is standing. Mix the cubed chicken, stock cube, mushrooms, sherry, flour, seasoning and cream together in a bowl. Add the drained pasta and mix in lightly. Microwave on Medium-High for 8–10 minutes. Sprinkle with the Parmesan, parsley and paprika, and serve.

COMBINATION OVEN: Cook at 200 °C and medium-low microwave power level for 12–14 minutes (20–25 minutes if your oven alternates between convection and microwave energy).

Brown Rice with Mushrooms (page 47) and Melanzane (page 47).

NOODLES, ONION AND SPINACH WITH CHEESE SAUCE

250 g/8 oz large pasta shells, cooked
 (see Pasta, page 43)
45 g/1½ oz butter
2 large onions, chopped
500 g/1 lb spinach, washed and
 coarsely chopped
salt and freshly ground black pepper to taste
500 ml/16 fl oz Cheese Sauce (page 44)
60 g/2 oz Cheddar cheese, grated
5 ml/1 teaspoon paprika

Cook the pasta. While the pasta is standing, place the butter and onions in a glass bowl and microwave on High for 3–4 minutes. Mix in the chopped spinach and seasoning, cover, and microwave on High for 5 minutes. Make the Cheese Sauce.

Place the pasta in a serving dish, top with the spinach mixture and pour the Cheese Sauce over. Top with grated cheese and paprika, then microwave on High for 3 minutes. Serve piping hot.

FETTUCINI WITH CREAMY BROWN MUSHROOM SAUCE

250 g/8 oz fettucini, cooked (see Pasta,
 page 43)
30 g/1 oz butter
5 ml/1 teaspoon dried rosemary
315 g/10 oz chestnut mushrooms, thinly sliced
1 clove garlic, crushed
250 ml/8 fl oz single cream
12.5 ml/2½ teaspoons Marsala
salt and freshly ground black pepper to taste
45 ml/3 tablespoons grated Parmesan cheese
15 ml/1 tablespoon snipped fresh chives

Cook the fettucini. While it is standing, make the sauce. Place the butter, rosemary and sliced mushrooms in a glass bowl and microwave on High for 4 minutes. Add the garlic, cream and Marsala, stir to combine, then microwave on Medium-High for 5 minutes. Season, then mix the mushroom sauce with the drained pasta and place the mixture in a casserole. Sprinkle with Parmesan cheese and snipped chives and serve piping hot.

BROWN RICE WITH MUSHROOMS

250 g/8 oz brown rice
5 ml/1 teaspoon salt
815 ml/26 fl oz vegetable stock
10 ml/2 teaspoons chopped fresh tarragon
250 g/8 oz chestnut mushrooms, sliced
1 green pepper, seeded and diced
12.5 ml/2½ teaspoons oil
30 g/1 oz butter
25 ml/5 teaspoons soy sauce
freshly ground black pepper to taste
30 g/1 oz chopped parsley
45 ml/3 tablespoons chopped spring onions
60 g/2 oz Pecorini cheese, grated

Microwave the rice, salt, stock and tarragon in a large bowl, covered, on High for 12 minutes, then on Medium-High for 30–40 minutes — until cooked. Stand for 15 minutes, during which time the liquid will be absorbed.

Microwave the mushrooms, green pepper, oil and butter in a bowl on High for 4–5 minutes, stirring halfway — until soft. Add the soy sauce and pepper. Stir into the rice with the parsley and onions. Sprinkle with cheese and microwave on High for 4–5 minutes to heat through.

MELANZANE

2 medium aubergines, thickly sliced
salt
45 ml/3 tablespoons oil
7.5 ml/1½ teaspoons chopped fresh basil
Homemade Tomato Sauce (page 9)
250 g/8 oz frozen creamed spinach,
    thawed and drained
250 g/8 oz mozzarella cheese, sliced
30 g/1 oz Parmesan cheese, grated
sprigs of fresh basil to garnish

Sprinkle the aubergine slices with plenty of salt, place in a colander and leave for 30 minutes. Rinse and dry.

Preheat a browning dish on High for 6 minutes. Add enough oil to cover the base of the dish. Add the aubergine (cook in batches) and microwave on High for 1 minute per side. Add more oil, if needed, during cooking. Drain the aubergine on paper towels. Layer half the aubergine, basil, sauce, spinach and cheeses in a casserole. Repeat the layers. Microwave, covered, on Medium-High for 10–12 minutes — until cooked. Garnish with basil and serve.

COMBINATION OVEN: Cook, uncovered, on 180 °C and medium-low microwave power level for about 15 minutes (25–30 minutes if your oven alternates between convection and microwave energy).

CHEESY VEGETABLE CASSEROLE

1 potato, peeled and thinly sliced
1 red onion, thinly sliced
4 courgettes, sliced
2 large carrots, peeled and thinly sliced
4 small squash, sliced
freshly ground black pepper to taste
220 g/7 oz Cheddar cheese, grated
30 g/1 oz butter
125 ml/4 fl oz yoghurt or soured cream

Layer the vegetables in a large casserole, sprinkle with black pepper and top with the cheese. Dot with the butter and pour the yoghurt or cream over. Microwave, covered, on Medium-High for 17 minutes. Uncover and microwave on Medium-High for another 5 minutes.

COMBINATION OVEN: Cook at 180 °C and medium-low microwave power level for 12–14 minutes (18–20 minutes if your oven alternates between convection and microwave energy).

VEGETABLE CURRY

Serve this delicious curry with Yellow Rice (page 13) and a selection of side dishes.

2 onions, thinly sliced
2 cloves garlic, crushed
30 ml/2 tablespoons oil
15–20 ml/3–4 teaspoons curry powder
5 ml/1 teaspoon turmeric
5 ml/1 teaspoon garam masala
5 ml/1 teaspoon grated fresh ginger
2 carrots, peeled and cubed
1 turnip, peeled and cubed
½ cabbage, shredded
salt and freshly ground black pepper to taste
250 ml/8 fl oz water
12.5 ml/2½ teaspoons chilli sauce
12.5 ml/2½ teaspoons cornflour
fresh coriander leaves to garnish

Microwave the onions, garlic and oil in a large glass bowl on High for 5–6 minutes. Stir in the curry powder, turmeric, garam masala and ginger. Microwave on High for 2 minutes. Add the vegetables and stir well. Microwave on High for 2 minutes. Add the seasoning and water. Microwave, covered, on High for 12–15 minutes — until the vegetables have softened. Add the chilli sauce and microwave on High for 3 minutes. (If necessary, mix the cornflour to a paste with a little water and stir in just before the end of cooking time.) Garnish and serve.

INDEX
•••••••••••••